THE 90-DEGREE TURN

Remaking Federal Government —
from Big, Bulky, and Misguided
to Lean, Decentralized, and Relevant

JB FRED EBERLEIN

Nemo propheta in patria

Thanks to Bobbie, a brother like no other.

And to the guardian of dialogue, my dad Jim.

TABLE OF CONTENTS

EPILOGUE

PREFACE
HOW DID THIS BOOK COME INTO BEING

I n 1975, I moved to Washington, DC, to start a graduate program at American University (AU) in the school of Public Administration. My goal was to become a civil servant, an employee of the Federal Government working for the American people. Having spent my third (junior) year in college studying in Europe, I imagined joining a foreign services agency. If not accepted by Department of State elites, I would look at positions in the CIA and elsewhere.

This all changed early in my program at AU when I was introduced to a philosophy that I found hard to embrace. In my graduate course in Government and Public Administration we were taught that *inflating* budgets was the path to success in the Federal Government. This was how a civil servant helped to build their agency and their position in it. Espoused by a professor who was also a high-ranking civil servant in the Department of Commerce, the idea was to make what could be a simple solution, a complex one.

Driving up costs was Washington's way of making the Federal Government bigger and grander. Results didn't matter as much as spending. Being a successful Federal Government employee meant building big, without consideration for how that might benefit, or rob, the country. The thinking was simple: why spend $1 when you can spend $10, $100, or $1,000? Why have a team of a few when it can be a team of thousands?

Ironically, a few years after dropping out of AU, I would find myself inside the Federal Government. Not as a civil servant but as a salesman of computer services and software. Now, the Government's practice of inflating budgets played to my advantage. I spent over ten years walking the halls of Federal Government agencies. Not just in Washington, but throughout the U.S. and in Europe. I sold to the Department of Defense (DoD), the National Aeronautics and Space Administration (NASA), the Nuclear Regulatory Commission (NRC), the National Institute of Standards and Technology (NIST), the National Security Agency (NSA), the U.S. Army Europe (USAREUR), NATO, and many other government agencies. I also learned the benefits of working with contractors and how they aid in Washington's non-stop big spend. I was one of thousands of salespeople chasing the billions of dollars that oozed out of Washington. Finding ways to exploit the bonanza of Federal Government spending was our specialty.

Maybe my sense of order and efficiency are too acute, but the extent of the Government's wastefulness bothered me, even when I was capitalizing on it. I could see that it was not sustainable. As with anything that grows uncontrollably, like cancer, it was apparent that Washington's spending habits would cripple the country, if not sink it. I began to realize that the United States of America was fine, but that the entity charged with running it was not. Washington was a dream world, filled with the aura of politics and a giddiness that comes with having money to burn.

Like many, I had resigned myself to the Federal Government's wasteful ways. Despite this, the thought of addressing this problem never escaped me. To this day, my interactions with the Federal Government as a U.S. citizen, taxpayer, and entrepreneur have only heightened my frustration and added to my determination to find an answer.

A few years ago, I had an epiphany. It came after reading Start-up Nation: The Story of Israel's Economic Miracle.[1] As one of many vignettes that underscore the book's theme, authors Dan Senor and Saul Singer relate a dispute at microchip manufacturer Intel Corporation. An argument between Intel HQ, in California, and Intel R&D, in Israel, had been raging for months.

Chip performance at Intel was measured in megahertz, the speed at which computer instructions are executed. To produce faster chips, Intel continuously needed to increase megahertz. This had been the practice for decades. But as chip speed increased, Intel was coming up against a problem: heat. With every increase in megahertz came a rise in temperature that threatened to melt the chip's interconnections and render it useless.

To address this problem, Intel R&D designed a new microarchitecture that performed better than previous chips while requiring no increase in megahertz. A win-win. But this was a problem for Intel HQ. Megahertz was the standard for determining a chip's worth. If megahertz didn't increase, how could Intel sell its chips? Time and again, Intel HQ would think the issue settled, only to have their Israeli counterparts relentlessly resurrect it.

Eventually, Intel HQ realized that a working chip was better than a fried one. Besides its brilliant engineers, what made Intel R&D Israel stand out was its determination. It was a striking example of the Israeli mindset and what makes for exceptional teams. Pointing

---

[1] *Start-up Nation: The Story of Israel's Economic Miracle* by Dan Senor and Saul Singer, 2008

out problems and arguing the facts took priority over hurting feelings or giving in to superiors. For a nation surrounded by existential threats, this personality trait is inherent in everyday life – whether defending the country or building a better fraud detection algorithm. In the end, Intel prospered. Not with a faster chip, but with a new chip architecture: the Pentium.

In Senor and Singer's book, Intel's transformation was described as a *right turn*. Reluctantly, Intel management realized it had to scrap its legacy megahertz outlook and reorient its thinking around performance. That lesson didn't come easily and was discomfiting to many who had to abandon old practices. In the end, Intel built on what they had developed over decades by leaving it behind. It was a bittersweet experience but a matter of necessity. Intel did the hard thing. They left the past, accepted a new future, and succeeded.

The Federal Government is the hub of the wheel that drives the U.S. That hub is fatigued, corroded, and showing significant stress. Washington can no longer manage the heavy workload placed upon it. It too needs a *right turn* –what I'm calling the 90-Degree Turn.[2]

This book puts forth a theory for executing the 90-Degree Turn in Washington, one that realigns central government with the needs of the country. Unproven, it will likely never work, particularly if we don't try. But what are our options? We're a bit like Intel. We either reinvent ourselves or go out of business. As a country, our situation is no different. It's just a matter of time.

---

[2] "The 90-Degree Turn" is apolitical. The idea of a "right turn" could be confused with the political right. For this reason, I replaced "right" with "90-Degree" in the hope of making it clear that the orientation of this book is neither right nor left nor in between.

While the focus of this book is on the U.S. Federal Government and its Congress, its principles can also be applied to state and local governments, as well as to any democratic government, including the European Union and its member states. The better we align all government with the needs of the country, the faster we can reduce waste and redundancy, streamline law and tax code, and return to the business of America.

Introduction

What can you expect from reading this book?

Efficiency is not in the interest of today's Federal Government. It flies in the face of Washington's top priority: spending. Not the disease but a symptom of it, spending is exacerbated by four characteristics of the Federal Government: age, complexity, size, and (fundraising-centric) politics. Together these four conditions define Washington's chronic, and worsening, underperformance. In this book I examine each of these and put forward a model for transitioning the Federal Government and renewing its purpose.

The envisioned model is not seen as a revolution but rather, as stated in the title, a turn, a pivot. Historically, revolutions outdo themselves and throw the baby out with the bathwater. However, as there are trillions of dollars of assets in the Federal Government, we need to protect Washington throughout the process of remaking it. Many of these assets are found in the Government's massive research archives and the collective brainpower that went into that research. Other assets include the know-how to manage our nuclear arsenal and the toxic waste that resulted from its production, as detailed in Michael Lewis's book The Fifth Risk.[3] We can also learn a lot from the Government's

---

[3] The Fifth Risk by Michael Lewis October 2, 2018

failures and take account of these failures; lessons learned are an asset too, provided we act on them.

The knock-on effects of age, complexity, size, and politics, thwart our ability to govern. If we measure Washington by its return-on-taxpayer-investment, we see performance that is scraping bottom and often negative. While industry has on-boarded lean management practices and recognizes that less is more, our central government remains stuck in the past.[4] A veritable monarch in its rigid top-down flow of money, policy, and power.

Productivity is optimized in small teams, not big ones. Already a fact before the internet boom, the effectiveness of small teams has only become more pronounced since. In the Federal Government new practices to address productivity are considered, evaluated, talked about, reported, and sometimes mimicked, but almost never implemented. It's the Washington way. Another chance to spend money on appearing efficient, while showing no evidence of it.

It's one example in thousands, albeit a trivial one. Have you ever tried logging into the My Social Security website in the early hours, perhaps to check your records? What do you see? This message: *"This service is not*

available at this time. Please try again during our regular service hours."

---

[4] With its origins in Japan, "[l]ean management is an approach to managing an organization that supports the concept of continuous improvement, a long-term approach to work that systematically seeks to achieve small, incremental changes in processes in order to improve efficiency and quality." Emily McLaughlin, TechTarget. August 2019

The world wide web is more than a quarter of a century old, but the Federal Government has yet to fully embrace it. While seeming to live in the modern world, Washington can't unglue itself from the past. This is partially the fault of civil servants, but more so the result of an old system that has enabled Washington to put politics ahead of best practices. It didn't start this way, but this is what it has become.

Age, complexity, and size provide camouflage to a political system incentivized to exploit its position in the Federal Government. When campaigning runs into the billions of dollars, reimbursement in the form of Government contracts or legislation, or both, should be expected. On this Washington has not failed.

According to the Federal Government website usaspending.gov, *"In Fiscal Year 2020, federal spending was equal to 31% of the total gross domestic product (GDP), or economic activity, of the United States that year ($21.00 trillion)."*[5] At thirty-one percent of GDP we, as a nation, have painted ourselves into a corner. We can't just slash budgets or scrap the Federal Government's massive bureaucracy. Doing either would seriously harm the economy and people alike.

So, what are the alternatives? Short of the Government's collapse, we don't seem to have a Plan B. The mission of this book is to begin the process of creating one.

---

[5] "How does federal spending compare to federal revenue and the size of the economy?" USAspending.gov Data Lab

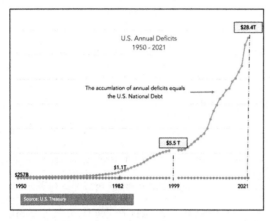

Federal Government reform should be imagined in the context of a sieve, not a hatchet. Talent and need must be meticulously separated from redundancy and waste. Today, we accept the unacceptable because we don't want to dwell on Washington's ineptitude. Despite this, we must acknowledge that we have a Federal Government that is consistently hemorrhaging money and underperforming like never before. Going from a national debt of $5.6 trillion in our first 200 years (1789-1999) to over $30 trillion in the past 20 years should sound alarm bells everywhere.[6] However, while the nation's ballooning debt is a problem, what should concern us most is the inefficiencies and systemic corruption that cause it.

This book provides a model for pivoting the U.S. Federal Government and returning it to its all-important role of serving the country. In this model, control over money is returned to state and local governments and taken away from Washington where, as we've seen, it is habitually and dangerously abused. The extent of this abuse goes beyond the country's bottom line and imposes hardships on people, stifles aspirations, and takes lives.

This doesn't mean that the Federal Government should no longer be funded. Of course, it must be, but as defined by local needs and not Washington's political agenda.

---

[6] U.S. Treasure. Fiscal Data. Historical Debt Outstanding (https://fiscaldata.treasury.gov/datasets/historical-debt-outstanding/historical-debt-outstanding).

In the 90-Degree Turn, we view Washington from the bottom-up rather than the top-down. This perspective serves as a means for identifying the Federal Government's most needed assets. It works as a filter for separating Washington overhead from Washington knowhow. Some might describe this as a form of direct democracy, but a better description is *applied democracy*. Making government dynamic; using what's needed and repurposing the rest.

Washington is a spending gusher whose top priority is to compensate campaign contributors and lobbyists alike. This is done to secure additional funds for future elections, for party and self. When not in the form of a contract award, payment is made indirectly through legislation.

The dedicated work of pharmaceutical lobbyists, supported by a war chest of cash, has robbed the country of billions. According to the Congressional Budget Office: "*The federal government is the largest purchaser of prescription drugs in the United States.*" Despite this, the agency that purchases medications for Americans, the Centers for Medicare & Medicaid Services (CMS), is prohibited by Congress from negotiating price. This is nothing new but has been the case for nearly 20 years since Medicare Part D legislation was passed by Congress in 2003.

Negotiating price based on volume is a standard part of doing business in the U.S. Walmart is a good example of this. They leverage their size, and the volume of goods they purchase, to drive down consumer prices. The power of this formula is evident in Walmart's success and the $514 billion in revenues generated in 2019.[7] However, unlike the fair market principles exercised by Walmart to drive down consumer prices, Congress

---

[7] Walmart 2019 Annual Report

prohibits CMS from negotiating with the pharmaceutical industry. The $370 billion spent by CMS on medications in 2019 was mostly at list price. This is the premium Americans pay for medicine. It's our involuntary donation to the pharma industry, in support of politicians. Thanks to the U.S. Congress, the wellbeing of 170 million Americans supported by CMS takes a backseat to campaign donations.

A 2021 article in STAT News reports that "*Seventy-two senators and 302 members of the House of Representatives cashed a check from the pharmaceutical industry ahead of the 2020 election …*"[8] In other words, more than two-thirds of Congressional members are accepting campaign donations from pharma lobbyists. Aided by Congress, CMS has been hijacked by the pharmaceutical industry.

In banking, hardworking lobbyists have ensured minimum balance and overdraft fees, a key source of bank profits and executive bonuses. According to Americans for Financial Reform (AFR), "*In the 2019–20 election cycle, Wall Street banks and financial services interests reported spending $2.9 billion to influence decision-making in Washington.*"[9] The same Congress that has driven the national debt to over $30 trillion doesn't seem to see the contradiction in disciplining the spending habits of everyday Americans. Congressional hypocrisy on high.

The Federal Government is bloated and broken. Through its calcified arteries runs a system of legal corruption. This is not a problem of political orientation – Republican, Democrat or Independent – but one of human nature. Spend enough time in Washington

---

[8] "More than two-thirds of Congress cashed a pharma campaign check in 2020, new STAT analysis shows." By Lev Facher. June 9, 2021. ("Pfizer's political action committee alone contributed to 228 lawmakers. Amgen's PAC donated to 218, meaning that each company helped to fund the campaigns of nearly half the lawmakers on Capitol Hill. Overall, the sector donated $14 million".)

[9] Wall Street Money in Washington 2019–2020 Campaign and Lobby Spending by the Financial Sector

and you'll find yourself bending to the sway of its money. It's nearly impossible to resist and works wonders in burying problems, not fixing them.

Money and the power that accompanies it are expected in Government. But it's the exploitation of that power through money that's central to the problem we face. For this reason, we need to recalibrate the flow of money to and from Washington. Beyond this, it would be logical to consider sweeping changes to all aspects of the Federal Government, including periodic updates to the Constitution, as envisioned by Thomas Jefferson. But that's another book on its own. The first order of business is to return Washington to its senses and make it accountable to the country.

At the heart of the 90-Degree Turn is a process for redefining the role and purpose of the Federal Government, while bringing it into the 21st century. As the creators of the world's first democratic republic, the U.S. is the guardian of its principles and compelled to act and correct course. Not just for the United States of America but for democracies around the world that have adopted the U.S. model. We can renew the American dream, and demonstrate the value of democratic government, by right-sizing our Federal Government while realigning it with the needs of the country.

In the modern age, we have learned that as organizations grow bigger and bigger, they become less and less productive. Typically, the benefits derived from the first one hundred employees is significantly greater than when an organization expands to two hundred employees. As groups grow beyond a certain size, returns diminish. Size goes from an asset to a liability. In a small group, everyone is more likely to have an intimate understanding of the mission, whether that's programming a gaming app or building a car. With this intimacy, insights are more likely to be identified, shared, seen as opportunities for improvement, and acted upon. In big organizations, like the Federal Government, this is much less likely to happen.

By adjusting the size of the Federal Government to conform with local needs, and drastically reducing the flow of money to and from Washington, we stop the loss of hundreds of billions of dollars. We also negate the corrosive power of money in politics and return value to government. Until this happens, our free fall continues. Rock-bottom is fast approaching.

1 BACKGROUND

A Brief Education in the Federal Government

As noted in the Preface, in the fall of 1975, I moved to Washington, DC, to attend graduate school at American University (AU). In one of my first classes in Public Administration, our professor, a high-ranking career civil servant from the Department of Commerce, posed a question.

He asked: "*If you're given a one-million-dollar budget, what do you do with it?*" One student asked what problem the one million dollars was intended to solve. The professor was quick to reply. "*The problem is irrelevant*," he said.

Another student suggested dividing the one million dollars into thirds: one third to study the problem, another to create a plan, and the last third to execute a solution. But this also didn't supply the answer the professor was seeking. "*What do you do with the one million dollars?*" he calmly repeated.

Not hearing more suggestions, the professor revealed the answer: "*Make the problem bigger and ask for ten million dollars. This is how you build your agency and your position in it.*"

Surprised by his answer, I thought it a joke at first. But as the professor continued, I realized this wasn't a joke but instead a recipe for how government bureaucrats should think. Whether a study on the cracking of eggs, a plan for better housing, or a mission to Mars, the key is to make everything bigger and more costly.[10] This was how model civil servants performed. In Washington, results were measured by budgets, not outcomes.

The professor exhibited no shame. He was open and honest, almost boastful. Efficiency was the domain of industry and those seeking profit; it had no place in our Federal Government. The mandate in Washington was to spend and spend big.

It was hard to accept the professor's perspective. It made no sense to my naive and unsophisticated mind. Solving problems didn't matter, but spending did? Being a worthy civil servant ran contrary to the outlook instilled in me at an early age by my Italian immigrant grandmother, Nana. She would say, "*Waste not, want not.*" In her eyes, wasting was as bad as wanting things you didn't need and couldn't afford. "*Waste not, want not*" wasn't just an expression but a lifestyle.[11] As the second of five children in a middle-class family living in upstate New York, Nana's edict was our eleventh commandment.

Not long into my graduate program, it all ended. I attended evening classes for a while only because I didn't want to give up too quickly. I was pretending to care about a degree

---

[10] National Institute of Health PubMed "Probability of an egg cracking during packing can be predicted using a simple non-destructive acoustic test." M M Bain, I C Dunn, P W Wilson, N Joseph, B De Ketelaere, J De Baerdemaeker, D Waddington

[11] Nana would hang used paper towels on the kitchen faucet to dry and reuse them later.

I didn't want. A career in the Federal Government wasn't for me. I thought: When did wasting money and putting a drag on productivity become the American way?

Little did I know at the time, but within a few years I would come to witness the inner workings of the Federal Government's spending habits. I would become one in an army of salespeople whose job it was to cash-in on Washington's spending addiction. We were commonly referred to as "*beltway bandits*" due to the offices we occupied along the 495 Beltway that surrounds Washington D.C. Feeding off a system that wanted to be fed upon was our specialty. The Federal Government was ripe for exploitation, and we were there to harvest it. My piece of the pie was a crumb compared to other forces that had gone from parasite to predator, taking Washington for all it's worth.

Mounting the Money Beast

In June 1978, my career in what we now call "tech" began. I was 25 and thrilled to be working for a recognized company: Control Data Corporation (CDC). A victim of tech's disruptive nature, CDC is today a dinosaur. But when I joined, it was a thriving international enterprise that employed over 50,000.

Competing against IBM, CDC shared in the new and booming data storage market that generated a billion dollars for the company in 1980. That represented one-third of CDC's total revenue; the rest came from the sale of CDC's Cyber computers, and from data services (Cybernet), where I worked. Known as *number-crunchers*, Cyber computers were designed to run scientific problems that required the handling of large amounts of data. IBM computers were great at managing ledgers and databases but struggled when it came to solving number-intensive problems. That was where CDC shone. Engineers, mathematicians, and scientists depended on Cyber computers to simulate a plane's fuselage for stress or calculate the optimal placement of fuel rods in a nuclear reactor. Even companies using IBM's most advanced computers would turn to CDC's Cyber computers for solving engineering problems.

At the National Bureau of Standards' sprawling campus in Gaithersburg, MD, building names read like a buyer's list for Cyber computers: Chemistry, Physics, Materials, Fire, Technology[12]. Most government agencies, however, couldn't afford a Cyber computer. Each cost millions of dollars to buy and millions to operate. But remote access to Cyber computers was cheap, and there were no fixed or upfront fees. Like a utility, charges were based on resources used.

Customers would visit one of CDC's four data processing centers in the U.S. or, as was becoming increasingly popular, they would connect via a conventional phone line. A user with a 1200 baud (1200 bits/second) connection was considered privileged in those days. Compared to today's firehose of internet bandwidth, 1200 baud was a trickle. But it was enough to enable users to interact with a remote computer and execute their programs.

There was no Graphical User Interface (outside of Xerox's PARC research lab, the idea of GUIs didn't yet exist). Looking into a computer monitor was about as entertaining as staring at an empty blackboard. Despite this, users were excited to compute from their offices. Long before the world wide web, computer networks were forming.

My job was to walk the halls of the government and sell access to Cyber computers. In addition to the Bureau of Standards, I also called on the Nuclear Regulatory Commission (NRC), and private companies such as Bechtel Power and NUS Nuclear Services (later

---

[12] The National Bureau of Standards changed its name to National Institute of Standards and Technology (NIST) in 1988.

acquired by Halliburton). I had no background in the sciences but spent my days introducing Cybernet to mathematicians and engineers. When the questions reached beyond my ken, which was often, I had access to an exceptional team of internal consultants. Many had backgrounds like the customers I was selling to. Without them I would have been lost and of no value to CDC.

I was excited to be in a company with so many smart, yet down-to-earth, people. It felt like a family. Our consultants did the heavy lifting. My job was to know the customer, get them to buy, and keep them happy.

Data services, or "*timesharing*" as it was then known, was a competitive market, but if you took care of your customers, they usually stayed with you. One of our competitors was Boeing; they were also a buyer of CDC Cyber computers used in the design and production of their aircraft. Despite their constant use, Boeing's expensive Cyber computers were not fully utilized. Wisely, Boeing created a timesharing division too, to sell access to its Cybers. While this offset the cost of Boeing's computers, it also created a competitor for CDC Cybernet. It took me a while to understand that it was in CDC's interest to sell computers to Boeing, even though Boeing competed with CDC's timesharing division. I remember this well. It awakened me to the complexities of the real world. Long before hearing the term *coopetition*,, I witnessed it.

Control Data was a turning point in my life, and I felt blessed. I was learning about something that interested me, computers, and settling into a great job with a recognized company at a time when employees and companies made lifetime commitments. "*Termination at will*" didn't exist in those happy times; it wasn't until I joined Oracle in 1989 that I first read those morally questionable words.

Sales Elites

Most memorable from my CDC days were the stories and lessons passed on from a handful of sales elites. Their success was demonstrated by the six-figure incomes they pocketed, the new Mercedes they drove, and the GQ dress code they faithfully adhered to.

It was perhaps my second week on the job when, full of ambition, I arrived early to work one morning. I thought the office would be empty. To my surprise, I found one of the sales elites, Bill, already at work. It was true; success doesn't come to the lazy. Hoping to start a conversation, I approached Bill in his office and asked: "*What's the best way to sell to the government?*" Without hesitation, Bill replied: "*Wire the spec. Now, get the fuck out of here and sell something!*"

Under normal circumstances, I may have asked a follow-up question, but it seemed a bad idea at the time. As I stood dumbfounded in the doorway to his office, Bill grabbed a bottle of mouthwash, took a gulp, gargled, and spit it onto the dark brown carpet that covered the office where it instantly disappeared. I thought, "Is this guy insane, or is this a hazing ritual?" Nervously, I smiled and moved on.

Perhaps it was the manner in which the insight was communicated, but it was a rule I came to live by: *wire the spec*, short for "*wire the specification.*" In other words, it was my job to work with civil servants to shape their requirements to CDC's advantage. Like lobbyists putting forth drafts of new legislation to members of Congress, we put forth technical requirements. Often this was done in the form of a *white paper.* Names, logos, and company references were removed. We wanted the white paper to look like it was produced by the agency we were trying to sell to.

Imagine taking a product or service, or even an idea, and putting it into a series of requirements that you hand over to a government employee. This is what we did to sell our goods. From our perspective, we were helping second-rate bureaucrats to act like first-rate businesspeople.

It was our litmus test. If all or most of the specification provided in our white paper appeared in the agency's public Request for Proposal (RFP), we knew we had a good chance of winning. If few or none of the specs appeared in the agency's RFP, we took that as a sign that the business wasn't ours. It was a loss, but we were spared the time that would have been wasted writing a proposal for an opportunity we wouldn't win. The ones that fell in between were the hardest to decide and the hardest to win. In these instances, we would try to beat the government at its own game by studying how it was weighing the evaluation.

The government's procurement process was a dreaded exercise for all parties involved. Agencies didn't like writing RFPs, and contractors didn't like responding to them. Just producing an RFP could take months. After it was released, public Q&A sessions were often held. We would get to see our competitors and hear their questions. Sometimes, in what appeared to be choreographed exchanges between contractors and end-user representatives (from the procuring agency), we would get a sense of the government's preferences.

For example, let's say the Department of Commerce wanted to upgrade its computer systems. Contrary to what consumers would do, Commerce is not allowed to shop around, find the computers they like, and buy them. Instead, Commerce is required to organize an internal committee to study the matter and draw up a list of requirements. This list might contain details of the computer's processing speed and storage capacity. It could also include conditions for support, repairs, and on-site consultations. In all, Commerce's requirements could run on for pages and include hundreds of items. In closely reviewing these details, one could narrow the field of likely bidders to a few. This, however, wouldn't stop others from trying to secure Commerce's business.

For every proposal received, the government had to invest hours evaluating and scoring each. Few responses were preferred to many, provided the agency's minimum (typically three) was reached. Our goal was to be one or none. Despite this outlook, too many of our RFP responses were guesswork. *"Throwing mud against the wall to see if it sticks,"* as my boss would say, was a hard way of learning. But many a newbie, myself included, did it anyway and hoped for the best. With failure I saw the necessity for finding better ways into the Federal Government's piggy bank.

From beginning to end, the RFP process could take over a year. It was a potential death sentence for salespeople and management who depended on meeting their annual quotas. You could win, but you might be well into your next job by then. Time, not competition, was our biggest enemy. Anything that could be done to reduce or circumvent the Government's procurement process increased the odds of success and hastened the payment of commissions. The Federal Government also preferred the circumvented approach; it provided an opportunity to spend more, faster, and with less interference.

Sometime after my first encounter with Bill, I recall him pulling a neatly folded single sheet of paper from his tailored suit jacket. It was a detailed breakdown of an RFP he was evaluating. Bill came from a time when handwriting was important; his was beautiful, almost art. The paper showed the RFP's evaluation criteria in detail. Bill was calculating how much importance the government attributed to the requirements given in the RFP.

By law, fifty-one percent of the government's decision had to be based on price. This left the balance of forty-nine percent open to the buyer's discretion. Bill had his peculiarities, but he knew how to work a government RFP. Not only could he wire a spec, Bill also knew how to unravel one, and use the government's complex procurement processes to his advantage.

The right government contracts could function as a Trojan horse that enabled companies to secure a position deep inside government agencies. Money might be lost initially, but those losses turned to profits as the winning contractor pushed through amendments for its goods and services and that of sub-contractors. Unlike RFPs, contract amendments could be processed in days. Breaking through to a government agency in this way could generate many years of predictable revenue and open up new business opportunities. It also gave contractors access to confidential information such as budgets, pending procurements, and details on competitors. In addition to the revenue generated from the contract and subcontracts, there was the possibility of getting a lot more.

Between the Federal Government's public procurements and the many contractors competing for government business, there existed a layer of espionage. In a world lacking in security and without the video surveillance cameras used today, engaging in illegal activities was easy. Secretaries, low-level administrators, and security guards were targets for bribes. All they had to do was pass on some information or look the other way. Help could be secured in exchange for lunch, dinner, an ounce of grass, sex, or friendship. A more serious request might be compensated with something bigger, like a new car.

This was the case when a couple of salesmen were given access late one night to the Department of Agriculture's procurement office. Prior to submitting their best-and-final offer, they wanted to know how their price compared to bids from competitors. The bribe worked. The salesmen found the information they wanted, adjusted their offer, and won the contract. And the security guard got a new car.

Exploitation for Good

Sadly, eight years after joining CDC, I watched it fall apart. Fortunately, there were other career opportunities, and in 1986 I was hired by the budding tech startup Alliant Computer. Alliant designed and built a new type of number-cruncher. It was air-cooled, less expensive to operate, and about one-twentieth the price of a CDC Cyber and other large, water-cooled supercomputers, like the Cray. Unlike my easier days at CDC, at Alliant I had to learn to think like an engineer. This was the mandate of CEO Ron Gruner, and cofounders Rich McAndrew and Craig Mundie. All were highly experienced engineers. It was an opportunity to learn how computers operated that I appreciate to this day.

Not long after its lofty debut on Wall Street, Alliant began its slide. There were already too many competitors in the super minicomputer niche, and new ones were still entering the market. It seems the brilliant engineers who were building ever faster air-cooled number-crunchers took little account of the market they were entering. Like Intel's dilemma, the focus on computer speed alone blinded many from seeing the bigger picture. It was a crowded market running on razor-thin margins. With the fall of the Berlin Wall, the market for super minicomputers collapsed. Government money earmarked for deterring the Soviet threat dried up quickly in the wake of the Cold War. In 1992, the same year that CDC ceased operations, Alliant went bankrupt.

Despite its continued disruptiveness, or maybe because of it, the tech industry was still expanding and there were many career opportunities to be realized. In 1990, I jumped from hardware to software, and from the relatively small market for scientific computing to the mass market for business solutions. I was hired by Oracle's Federal Division in Bethesda, Maryland, and was responsible for sales to the Office of the Secretary of Defense, i.e., the Pentagon.

I was thrilled to be working at Oracle. The money was great, as were the people and the parties. Selling hardware was hard. Selling software was considerably easier and much more lucrative.

Finding civil servants who wanted our products or services didn't always assure us of getting their business. In addition to dragging on for months, the government's publicly advertised proposals attracted competitors. A far better approach was to work with companies that had *Trojan horse* contracts in place.

I utilized this method twice during my first year at Oracle, working separately with defense manufacturing giant Grumman and the communications titan ConTel.[13] Each had large service contracts with the Pentagon. The sale through Grumman netted Oracle $250,000, and the one with ConTel, which came on the last day of Oracle's fiscal year, netted $650,000. Both contractors pocketed large commissions. It was their undisclosed transaction fee for owning a pipeline to the Pentagon's bank account.

Everybody was happy, including the Department of Defense. It was a chance to spend that required little work. Only a contract amendment was needed. It was astonishing how government buying practices varied so drastically. At one end of the spectrum: a detailed specification and publicly issued RFP that could take a year to produce, collect, evaluate,

---

[13] ConTel Corporation (Continental Telephone) was the third largest independent phone company in the United States prior to the 1996 telecom deregulation. It was acquired by GTE in 1991. In 2000, GTE was acquired by Verizon.

and award for any purchase of $50,000 or more. At the other end: a contract amendment that could be processed in days, required no evaluation, and had no limit. That's the Federal Government. From elaborate and detailed to simple and silly. Imbalanced, convoluted, and vulnerable.

Helping to exploit the Government's spending habits was a growing ecosystem of contractors who embraced their work enthusiastically. The money was excellent, and there was little chance of it running out. Changes occurred depending on political influence or foreign conflict, but the money never stopped. Privately, some of us resented civil servants and saw them as lazy second-rate citizens looking for an easy paycheck that they would otherwise have to earn in the private sector. As employees of a for-profit company, we considered ourselves smarter and harder workers.

Federal employees were also union members. Short of a criminal act, the threat of termination didn't exist for them. In the private sector it was the opposite. Employment contracts at Oracle and other tech companies now read *"termination-at-will."* We could be fired at any time and for any reason. This meant two-weeks' severance pay and fifteen minutes to pack your belongings. It was the price for missing quota, not being liked, or being on the wrong side of an argument. We lived by our convictions; civil servants lived by their fears. Or so we thought.

The reality was that many civil servants suffered more than salespeople in their everyday struggle with regulations that slowed their work and dampened their enthusiasm. In the end, we collaborated. The civil servant relied on the contractor to get what they needed, and the contractor relished the opportunity to apply their magic and rake in the commissions that followed.

What I witnessed was a tiny slice of a much bigger problem that has only grown worse over time. On emotionally charged political issues like the 2003 invasion of Iraq, or the 2013 implementation of Healthcare.gov, contractors showed their mastery at milking the Federal Government's reckless spending habits. In Iraq, a non-competed contract was awarded at the direction of Vice President Cheney to the company he previously headed, Halliburton. Cheney's tenure at Halliburton wasn't particularly stellar, but he made up for that during his time as Vice President. The Pentagon negotiated a cost-plus-award-fee (CPAF) contract with Halliburton. Made illegal as a result of World War One profiteering, the CPAF contract was revived in time for the Vietnam war.

Under a CPAF agreement, contractors are reimbursed for the cost of the goods they purchase in support of the awarded contract. On top of this they are paid a fee for their services. It sounds fair, right? Well, it is fair provided it's not abused. But there's an Achilles heel to the CPAF approach. If costs aren't capped, as was the case with the Halliburton contract, one can spend without limits. Rather than searching for the best deals to serve the U.S. military and the American people, Halliburton sought out the most expensive. Instead of replacing an air filter in a new long-haul truck that was clogged because of desert sand, Halliburton would burn the truck and order a replacement. Award fees added up quickly. Service members were required to give their laundry to Halliburton sub-contractors at a cost to taxpayers of $100 per bundle. Dissatisfied with the results, service personnel asked if they could do their own laundry, at a cost of $5 per bundle. The Department of Defense would have none of it. Saving taxpayer money was never their thing.

When it came to providing transportation for officers and other personnel, Halliburton acquired top-of-the line SUVs, for a war zone. To bolster fees, vehicles were leased, as this provided the costliest way of obtaining them and the most profit for Halliburton.

Shareholders benefited at the cost of taxpayers thanks to Mr. Cheney, who not only secured the Halliburton contract but also defended it. Despite reports early in the war of money spent in violation of Halliburton's contract, nothing was done.[14] Ten years after the March 2003 invasion of Iraq, and long after Mr. Cheney left Washington, it was estimated that Halliburton had been *"awarded at least $39.5 billion in federal contracts."*[15]

Big spending was the mandate from day one of the Affordable Care Act (ACA), not because the ACA required it but because the political spotlight did. In Washington, one hundred million dollars ($100,000,000) is pocket change. The initial budget of $93,700,000 would have been more than enough to fund the Health and Human Service (HHS) health insurance marketplace, Healthcare.gov. However, when launched in October 2013, the cost of Healthcare.gov was $634,000,000: nearly seven times its initial budget. It was the world's most expensive website – not by percentage but by orders of magnitude. Ten months after its launch, the Inspector General for HHS reported that costs for Healthcare.gov had risen to $1.7 billion.[16] *Eighteen times* its original budget. We can be assured another billion or more has been spent maintaining Healthcare.gov since.

As with Halliburton, CPAF contracts were instrumental in the big spend on Healthcare.gov. The title of the IG's report tells it all: *"An Overview Of 60 Contracts That Contributed To The Development And Operation Of The Federal Marketplace."* Sixty contractors working on a single project is a surefire recipe for reckless spending and poor performance. But this is how Washington likes it. Not lean management, but the opposite. Not gradual steps, but all at once. Like trying to build a mansion, not in a year but in an afternoon.

---

[14] Pentagon Finds Halliburton Overcharged on Iraq Contracts. New York Times by Douglas Jehl. Dec. 11, 2003.

[15] "Contractors Reap $138 billion from Iraq war." Anna Fifield. Financial Times. March 18, 2013.

[16] Department of Health and Human Services OFFICE OF INSPECTOR GENERAL. Daniel R. Levinson. August 2014 OEI-03-14-00231

Healthcare.gov is a Federal Government trifecta. First, we pay top dollar for a site that doesn't work. We then pay to fix that site. Finally, we pay for the IG to investigate what went wrong. Another report to nowhere is written and stored on a government bookshelf. There's a brief consideration of lessons learned and maybe a congressional hearing. Then it's back to business as usual.

Rather than managing resources and funds intelligently, the Federal Government looks for every opportunity to spend – not usually out of evil intent, but out of bad habit. Notwithstanding the services provided to Americans, the cost of Healthcare.gov underscores the extent of Federal Government waste and mismanagement. Website development experts familiar with the sophistication of Healthcare.gov estimated its real cost to be in the range of $4 to $5 million. The most expensive websites prior to Healthcare.gov didn't cost more than $10 million.

Giving Washington the benefit of doubt, let's assume $10 million is a conservative benchmark for developing a complex website like Healthcare.gov. Using this figure, we can arrive at an empirical measurement of the Federal Government's inefficiency. At $1.7 billion, Healthcare.gov cost 170 times what it should have.[17] Looked at another way, for every $1.00 of taxpayer money spent on Healthcare.gov, about half a penny ($.0058) of value was received in return. If cars were manufactured with the same inefficiency as Healthcare.gov the cost of a $22,000 Ford would be $3,960,000.[18]

---

[17] $1,700,000,000 / $10,000,000 = 170

[18] "How Much Does It Actually Cost Manufacturers to Make a Car?" by Britta Cross. July 22, 2019. LLCTLC. Note: The cost of a $22,000 Ford is estimated to be $20,000. For every dollar paid for the Ford the buyer is receiving $.91 in value. As the value for Healthcare.gov is $.005 for every dollar paid its relative cost to the Ford is calculated as $.90 divided by $.005 = 180 * $22,000 = $3,960,000.

How effectively taxpayer money is spent was never a concern in Washington. Budgets are imagined as swimming pools where it's the Federal Government's job to drain that pool every year while pushing for a bigger one for next year. This philosophy is not questioned but instead embraced by all who participate in Washington's big spend. The Congressional Budget Office (CBO) and the Government Accountability Office (GAO), agencies whose job is to guard against reckless spending, serve as little more than window-dressing, creating the illusion of money well managed.

Complexity is baked in. As in the dark world of money laundering, complexity – *layering* – is used by Congress to conceal how money is spent. When elections require billions to finance, there is a price to be paid. This should be a surprise to no one.

Further proof of the Federal Government's bloated state is apparent when asking a simple question, like *"How many people work for the Federal Government?"* Washington's answer is found in a 10-page report titled *"Federal Workforce Statistics Sources: OPM and OMB."*[19] In the introduction, we learn that the Federal Government's accounting of employees is not easy to follow:

> *"Sources may vary in their totals due to differences in how federal workforce statistics are compiled. Some sources rely on 'head counts' of employees (OPM), some on total hours worked (such as the Office of Management and Budget), some on surveys of employing agencies, and others on self-identification by workers surveyed in their homes."*

After a mind-numbing comparison of headcount methodologies used by OPM and OMB, we finally arrive at an answer on page 4 in *"Table 2. Federal Civilian Employees*

---

[19] Federal Workforce Statistics Sources: OPM (Office of Personnel Management) and OMB (Office of Management and Budget). Updated October 24, 2019."

On-Board Personnel, 2012-2018."[20] The answer: 2,100,802 as of 2018. However, just below this table there's a note stating that many entities of the Federal Government are omitted from the headcount.

"Current coverage does not include:
> *Board of Governors of the Federal Reserve*
> *Central Intelligence Agency*
> *Defense Intelligence Agency*
> *Foreign Service personnel at the State Department*
> *National Geospatial-Intelligence Agency*
> *National Security Agency*
> *Office of the Director of National Intelligence*
> *Office of the Vice President*
> *Postal Regulatory Commission*
> *Tennessee Valley Authority*
> *U.S. Postal Service*
> *White House Office*
> *Foreign Nationals Overseas*
> *Public Health Service's Commissioned Officer Corps*
> *Non-appropriated fund employees*
> *Selected legislative branch agencies, the judicial branch, or the military. "*

In all, there are sixteen exceptions to the Government's headcount. Likely, there's a report somewhere in the Federal Government explaining this, too.

The complexity involved in calculating the Government's headcount is by design. Washington doesn't know its actual size and finds it too difficult to come up with an answer. The individuals who produced the Federal Workforce Report are likely intelligent and dedicated civil servants and contractors. Presumably, based on my own experience, they are a cheerful bunch and proud of their work. But the concept of simplifying things is just not in their job description. To the contrary, each is out to prove their smarts by adding to the Government's labyrinth of all things complex. Among colleagues in the Federal Government, the OPM and OMB report might be seen as a masterpiece. Unfortunately, to the rest of the country, it reads like the mumbo-jumbo of the elite: *"Hey taxpayer, aren't you impressed with how clever we are? Complexity is a mandate we're happy to uphold. No cost should be spared in its pursuit."*

In 2010, I attained a small business grant from the National Institute of Health (NIH) for $250,000. Three years prior I had launched a healthcare company, ReliefInsite, that provided a secure online HIPAA-compliant service for patients to track and report their pain. Under the NIH grant we would enhance the body maps in our app for use in acupuncture. The new push at NIH was in Complementary and Alternative Medicine (CAM), and we were happy for an opportunity to expand on the functionality of our service. Receiving payment was easy, but no one from NIH ever checked our work. For all they knew we were playing video games instead of developing the service we promised. Despite talk of bringing new solutions to market, I learned from our NIH project coordinator that he was too busy issuing new grants to pay any attention to existing ones. CAM, which had been a hot item at NIH the previous year, fizzled as new spending opportunities emerged.

While surveying the market in preparing our grant proposal, I learned that some companies made it their practice to milk NIH and other government agencies that offered small business grants. It was widely recognized that Washington's top priority was to empty their budgets. To this end, some contractors helped by submitting small business grant proposals at every opportunity. Whether any work was done or not didn't seem to matter, and NIH didn't seem to care. Wordsmithing a previous submission and populating it with the latest NIH buzz words was the ticket to easy money. Of all the small companies that should have benefited from these grants, only a tiny minority did. That minority was made up of teams that were persistent and skilled at exploiting the Federal Government's small business funds.

Reflecting on this experience after our grant ended, I couldn't imagine investors of venture capital or seed funding behaving like NIH. Real investors will *always* keep a close eye on how their money is spent. Washington couldn't afford this level of attention. Its obsession with spending prevented any assessment of results. Every couple of months during the grant, I would receive an email from somewhere in the Federal Government asking if there had been any reports of discrimination or sexual harassment. Fortunately, I had none to report. Unfortunately, this was the full extent of the Federal Government's follow-up. Money was spent and nothing was accomplished. Governmental utopia.

Misguided War

Some patriotic Americans take exception to this topic. They feel war is a necessity that brings value over the long term. This outlook could be correct; I would argue it isn't. Nevertheless, the point here is not one of patriotism but of bloated budgets. While the big spend that is Washington has made it possible to build a massive military, money has also corrupted that military.

Not just wasteful, the Federal Government's spending habits set the stage for bad outcomes and negative returns to taxpayers. Chief among these is misguided war. Thousands of companies, big and small, depend on defense spending. At 732 billion dollars annually, defense is the biggest slice of the U.S. economy. It's three times China's and over eleven times Russia's military spend.[21]

---

[21] The 15 countries with the highest military spending worldwide in 2019. Statista
https://www.statista.com/statistics/262742/countries-with-the-highest-military-spending/

Where's the premium for hard work, innovation, and technological achievement – all in a vast land far removed from harm? It is negated by an oversized defense budget that demands a national sense of paranoia to justify it. The effect is one of perpetual war, at home and abroad. The more the Federal Government seems determined to protect us, the more skeptical we become. Increasingly, Washington sounds like the Russian mafia, creating the very danger they claim to protect us from.

Defense, and the moral use of force, is vital to the preservation of democracy. However, defense spending should be weighed in proportion to other priorities. Real threats to the country are drowned out by maintaining a heightened defense posture. Basic needs, like infrastructure, are easy to push aside when fear strikes. Initially, fears are based on fact, but invariably those facts take on a spin of their own driven by political calculation. This is not the work of the deep state, unauthorized and hidden from the public, but rather our everyday way of churning the mill of astronomical and counter-productive defense spending.[22]

It's a vicious cycle of which Vietnam and Iraq are victims. Both started with justifiable fears: the spread of communism and weapons of mass destruction, respectively. Yet, both ended in disaster. Other than a demonstration of military might, these wars produced only destruction, misery, and cost. If they have any value, it's in the lessons they try to teach us. But, under the pressure to keep spending, the urge to ignore those lessons is strong. It's easier to yank the chain of patriotism and watch the country quake, than to trim defense spending.

---

[22] $753,000,000,000 is the FY2021 defense budget.

Oversized military budgets gave us Vietnam and blinded us from our reasons for being there. Expending lives and money was simpler than admitting a mistake that could tarnish the American brand. A decade before the war ended, Undersecretary of Defense John McNaughton made clear why the U.S. continued to fight:

> 70% - To avoid a humiliating U.S. defeat.
> 20% - To keep SVN [South Vietnam] and adjacent territory from Chinese.
> 10% - To permit the people of SVN to enjoy a better, freer way of life.[23]

In Vietnam, oversized budgets worked against the U.S. rather than in support of it. A lesser nation would have been forced to think and act more wisely.

Bloated budgets are the source of our misguidedness. The rivalry between the Central Intelligence Agency and the Department of State provides evidence of this. Twenty months prior to 9/11, in January 2000, while spying on a meeting in Malaysia, the CIA identified Khalid al-Mihdhar as an al-Qaida operative. The CIA also knew that al-Mihdhar had a multiple-entry visa to the U.S. Yet, it wasn't until August 23, 2001, nineteen days before the 9/11 attacks, that the CIA placed al-Mihdhar on the State Department's watch list.[24] Putting competition before cooperation, the CIA aided terrorist al-Mihdhar in the crashing of American Airlines flight 77 into the Pentagon. Twenty months, 586 days, had elapsed before the CIA shared its knowledge with State. Thinking of 9/11 as a ticking timebomb with one hour till detonation, the CIA's delay took over 58 minutes off the clock. September 11, 2001 could have been prevented in a functioning government, but not one so overbudgeted that it worked against itself.

Oversized budgets were in play during the second Gulf War, which started with the invasion of Iraq in March 2003. Many argued that Hussein needed to be taken out. It's

---

[23] Source: Department of State, Vietnam Negotiating Files: Lot 69 D 412, Project Mayflower. Top Secret; Sensitive. Copies were sent to McGeorge Bundy, Unger, McNamara, and Vance. March 10, 1965.

[24] "September 11 and the Adaptation Failure of U.S. Intelligence Agencies." By Amy B. Zegart. International Security Vol. 29, No. 4 (Spring, 2005), pp. 78-111 (34 pages)

not that this thought never occurred to George H.W. Bush (Bush Sr.) during the first Gulf War (1990-1991). However, as one with significantly more experience than his son, Bush Sr.'s mind ventured beyond impulse. He had learned to question things. He thought: *Isn't the enemy (Iraq) of our enemy (Iran) a vehicle for checking power in the middle east? What happens if Hussein is removed; how can we be sure his successor won't be worse?*

Those questions occurred to a man who had experienced war and had been shot down in the Pacific during World War Two. In a crew of three he was the only to survive. "*With the wings of his plane on fire and smoke pouring into the cockpit, future President George H.W. Bush parachuted into the Pacific Ocean, where he floated for hours on a life raft, vomiting uncontrollably and bleeding profusely from his forehead.*"[25]

Unlike his son, Bush Sr. understood the importance of approaching war with a clear head. He made decisions cautiously knowing there would always be things he didn't know. His son, and the team that would sell the country on the necessity to invade Iraq, were sure of their arguments. What was there to question about CIA Director George Tenet's "slam dunk" assertion that Iraq possessed weapons of mass destruction (WMDs)? Having played it out in their imaginations a thousand times, the Iraq invasion would be the crowning achievement of the Bush Jr. presidency. Long before it ended, we celebrated "Mission Accomplished" for an operation that was far from it.

Despite credible indications to the contrary, it was argued that Hussein had a role in 9/11 and worked with Bin Laden. That was obvious to 95% of Americans. So, it became a fact even though it wasn't. It was a fact of convenience that many still believe today. Reports

---

[25] "George H.W. Bush's Role in WWII Was Among the Most Dangerous" Jesse Greenspan. February 13, 2019. History.com

from within intelligence agencies, including the CIA, told a different story. Bin Laden detested Hussein and operated on his own.

Four hundred billion dollars ($400,000,000,000) budgeted annually for thousands of defense contractors and another fifty-five billion ($55,000,000,000) in defense exports makes war inevitable. [26] [27] Military action is easy in a world of oversized budgets and lethal weapons when mixed with misguided politics that removes the need to think critically. Where *certainty* rules, there is no interest in questioning assumptions; better to call them facts.

In his book, Thinking, Fast and Slow, behavioral economist and Noble Prize recipient Daniel Kahneman explains that the slow part of the brain, where thinking happens, is not called upon when one is *slam dunk* sure. However, easy answers often equate to wrong ones. This is the domain of our trigger finger brain: quick and dirty, but usually incorrect. Insight, and decision-making, are found in the brain's lazier and slower counterpart, where thinking takes place. Thinking is hard work that many work hard to avoid.

The 1962 Cuban Missile Crisis ended without a casualty in part because it wasn't a slam dunk. On the brink of nuclear war, Kennedy and his administration were under enormous pressure. They had to think hard and be clever. Despite the U.S.'s military might, brains ultimately saved the day. Air Force General Curtis E. LeMay argued that it was time to take out the Russian nuclear arsenal. Kennedy, whose war experience was as traumatic as Bush Sr's, took a different course. He and his team imagined themselves in Khrushchev's shoes. Then, they cherry-picked the Kremlin's communications, negotiated the removal

---

[26] Bloomberg Government. Posted June 26, 2020 https://about.bgov.com/top-defense-contractors/

[27] Defense One "The U.S. Exported Arms Worth $55B in the Past Year" M Weisgerber, October 15, 2019

of missiles from Cuba, and averted war. It was an extremely tense period that involved many highly sensitive decisions. Nothing about it was *slam dunk* other than the fear it caused at home and around the world.

So great is the urge to spend that any attempt at savings is ignored and hidden with the Pentagon's waste. A December 5, 2016, story in *The Washington Post* by Craig Whitlock and Bob Woodward shows the extent of the abuse.

"The Pentagon has buried an internal study that exposed $125 billion in administrative waste in its business operations amid fears Congress would use the findings as an excuse to slash the defense budget, according to interviews and confidential memos obtained by The Washington Post.

The report, issued in January 2015, identified 'a clear path' for the Defense Department to save $125 billion over five years. The plan would not have required layoffs of civil servants or reductions in military personnel. Instead, it would have streamlined the bureaucracy through attrition and early retirements, curtailed high-priced contractors and made better use of information technology.[28] "

Fiscal mismanagement to this degree – $125,000,000,000 – is the result of a system unwilling to control its gluttony. It sounds an alarm. Not just for its wastefulness, but because of the bad decisions that result from wastefulness.

Oversized budgets create the illusion of overwhelming military might. While it may be comforting to some, it blinds us. It makes aggression too easy and removes the necessity

---

[28] "Pentagon buries evidence of $125 billion in bureaucratic waste" December 5, 2016 Whitlock and Woodward

for examining alternatives. In a *might makes right* world, choices are narrowed, not broadened. In Kahneman's field of behavioral economics, this is known as the *availability bias*, and it's the cause of many bad decisions. In the entangled web of money, military, and politics, this bias is usually evident from the outset when it's said that "*all options are on the table.*" Many read this as code for saying that war is not just a consideration but a preference.

To address this problem, while defense remains centralized in the 90-Degree Turn, defense funding should be determined locally. In this way, defense spending is looked at in proportion to other needs. The lobbyists that lurk Pentagon and Capitol halls work against proportionality. They're paid to bolster spending, not to bring value. Breaking through this problem requires removing Washington's control over taxpayer dollars. What Congress did with relative efficiency in the country's first two centuries has fallen off the rails in the new millennium, with defense spending leading the way.

At a local level, questions like the need for another stealth bomber will be considered more rationally than in Washington. As the U.S. is estimated to have 540 stealth warplanes to China's 41 and Russia's 10, the logic of building another is not a topic for discussion in Washington.[29] Today, that determination is political and buried in budgets that are hidden from the public. De-centralized local decision-making is less likely to be highjacked by lobbyists. By reversing the flow of money and decisions from top-down to bottom-up, Washington is brought in line with the country. In time, balance and order are restored.

---

[29] "How Many Stealth Warplanes Are There In The World—And Who Has Them?" David Axe. Forbes. July 1, 2020.

There will be many challenges to implementing the 90-Degree Turn. The biggest is an unwillingness to act. The status quo is fine, until it isn't. We have now reached this point.

2 WHAT AILS THE FEDERAL GOVERNMENT

Government Wrapped in Government

E very minute of every day, the Federal Government faces challenges at home and abroad. In addition to this, it needs to think ahead and plan for the unexpected. Under optimal circumstances, this workload is substantial; burdened by a colossal bureaucracy, it's made enormous. Add in the influence of fundraising-centric politics, and it becomes impossible.

America is not alone. Despite its young age, complexity, size, and politics are also problems for the European Union (EU) and contributed to BREXIT, the United Kingdom's decision to leave the EU.

Political fundraising is not the problem in the EU that it is in the U.S. However, like the U.S., the EU's operating costs are disproportional to the benefits provided. Additionally, according to the Greens/EFA parliamentary group between "*€179 billion and €950 billion*" is lost each year to corruption in the EU's top-down management of money.[30]

Even more is lost to organized crime. According to an EU Briefing from 2021 these losses are "*estimated at between €218 billion and €282 billion annually*".[31]

Founded in 1991, the EU government is an infant compared to the U.S. Made by governments for government, the EU missed an opportunity to create a modern, technology-driven, lean government. While exhibiting many of the bad traits found in the U.S. Federal Government, the EU hasn't had the time to mature to the level of excess found in Washington.

As an economic and security block, the European Union is good for Europe and the world. But its execution is hampered by a centralized approach that, like Washington, is inefficient and out of touch. People may have the best intentions but consume a lot to produce little. Outcomes vary from terrible, as in the COVID vaccine roll-out of 2021, to disastrous, as in the Syrian mass migration of 2015. Like the U.S. Federal Government, sub-par is *situation normal* in the European Union.

The European Union's dual centers lay 440 kilometers (273 miles) apart and testify to the EU'S affinity for putting process before productivity. Sessions of the EU's 705-member Parliament are held in Strasbourg, France. However, committee meetings –

---

[30] The cost of corruption across the EU. The Greens/EFA Group. 2018.

[31] Understanding the EU response to organized crime.

where legislation is formed – take place in Brussels, Belgium. In all, the cost to European taxpayers is €114 million annually.[32]

Worse, by European standards at least, is the environmental impact. *"Despite claiming to be a carbon-neutral institution, Parliament's 12 annual trips to Strasbourg are estimated to emit between 11,000 and 19,000 tonnes of CO2 emissions per year."*[33]

Government wrapped in government is not a plan for the future. Although the UK campaign to leave the EU was based on lies and patriotic gibberish, Britain's frustration with the entanglement of EU rules and regulations was understandable. After a while, people burn out. They simply want to return to what they're familiar with, for better or worse. It's no different in the U.S.

Like the need for the 90-Degree Turn in Washington, there are calls in the EU for a bottom-up approach to government. In September 2018, European economic thinktank Bruegel.org published a policy brief: *"One Size Does Not Fit All: European Integration By Differentiation."*[34] Bruegel advocates for *"a 'bare bones EU' built around the customs union and the single market, together with a set of vital policy matters, such as trade relations and the EU budget."*[35] Unlike the financial problems facing Washington, the issues driving the need for a bottom-up approach in the EU are political. The top-down approach of the European Council on sensitive matters, like integration, are *"often not delivering results."*[36]

---

[32] EU parliament's €114m-a-year move to Strasbourg 'a waste of money', but will it ever be scrapped? By Lauren Chadwick. Updated: 20/05/2019

[33] "MEPs reiterate call for single seat for Parliament." The Parliament Magazine. By Martin Banks. 04 Dec 2019

[34] Policybrief (Issue 3) September 2018 By Maria Demertzis et.al. Breugel.org

[35] "Improving the efficiency and legitimacy of the EU: A bottom-up approach" by Merler, Tagliapietra, Terzi and Bruegel. October 9, 2018

[36] Policy brief (Issue 3) September 2018 by Maria Demertzis et.al. Breugel.org

The challenges faced in the U.S. are, in many respects, much greater than those faced in Europe. In the context of the 90-Degree Turn, these challenges have been narrowed to *age, complexity, size,* and *politics*. While addressed individually in the following pages, each should be seen as threads and not silos. Age is interwoven with complexity, as complexity is interwoven with size.

Age

The age of our government and its life expectancy are seldom discussed. If we draw a reference, it's usually to past kingdoms like the Roman Empire or, more recently, the British Empire. But there is no reference point for the radical departure from the old-world's strict hierarchical order of Rome and Britain to the democratic republic conceived and implemented by the Founding Fathers. They debated and drafted the Articles of Confederation (and later the Constitution) *not* just to free the colonies from British rule, but also to replace an old and repressive model of government with a new and liberating one. The new model of *"We the people"* offered freedoms, justice, and prosperity not afforded to ordinary people in the old world. It may sound mundane today, but in the 18th Century it was radical, and it worked. As proof of its success, over half of the world's countries have since adopted the democratic model that originated in the U.S.[37]

Well-read and great thinkers, the Founding Fathers drew on their collective knowledge of history. They studied the classics and debated the objections to democracy expressed by Socrates 2,000 years prior. Their view wasn't just an American view but a world view. They understood that to create a better system of government for the future, it was essential to understand mistakes from the past. It's because of their rigor, broad thinking,

---

[37] "Despite global concerns about democracy, more than half of countries are democratic" May 14, 2019. Pew Research Center.

and determination that the United States came into existence. No doubt, the threat of being captured, tried for treason, and hung by the British was an incentive to get it right.

With age, we inherit the relics of past laws, regulations, code, policy, and politics. Decisions, many of which are irrelevant today, remain as cogs in the Federal Government's grinding wheel of diminishing returns. The notion of starting anew from a blank slate is not an aspect of our democratic model. Had the Founding Fathers been afforded the insights into organizational management that we have today, they may have added an Article to the Constitution mandating periodic streamlining of laws, regulations, code, and policy.

Thomas Jefferson was the exception. Six months after the U.S. Federal Government began operation, in September 1789, while in France, he expressed his concern in a letter to James Madison: "*The question whether one generation of men has a right to bind another, seems never to have been started either on this or our side of the water.*" In detail, Jefferson outlined his thoughts on the topic, adding: "*No society can make a perpetual constitution, or even a perpetual law.*"

In July 1816, years after his presidency, in a letter to Virginia lawyer and historian Samuel Kercheval, Jefferson's farsighted thinking reflects his brilliance: "*Some men look at constitutions with sanctimonious reverence, and deem them like the ark of the covenant, too sacred to be touched.*" "*Laws and institutions,*" he wrote, "*must go hand in hand with the progress of the human mind. As that becomes more developed, more enlightened, as new discoveries are made, new truths disclosed, and manners and opinions change with the change of circumstances, institutions must advance also, and keep pace with the times.*"

Jefferson thought beyond his time and accepted the limitations of his own experience. To Kercheval, he wrote: "*It* [the past] *was very like the present, but without the experience of the present.*" More than his contemporaries, Jefferson understood that change was both good and inevitable and that resisting it was problematic. Arguing this point, he correctly predicted the fall of European kingdoms that came a century later, writing: "*Their monarchs, instead of wisely yielding to the gradual change of circumstances, of favoring progressive accommodation to progressive improvement, have clung to old abuses, entrenched themselves behind steady habits…*"

Although he wouldn't experience the industrial revolution that began soon after his death, Jefferson was ready for it and the technological revolution that would shape the twentieth century. He understood ignorance – his own and others – and advocated for the evolution of government where insights and learnings could be harvested to further the cause of democracy. The concept of lean management didn't exist in Jefferson's day. Nevertheless, we can imagine him studying it and applying its principles to the Federal Government.[38]

Complexity

When Dr. Benjamin Franklin said, "*Never confuse motion with action,*" he must have been peering into his crystal ball and seeing the future of the Federal Government. Franklin was a man of action who kept a strict schedule, starting every day at 5 A.M. Given his many and varied accomplishments, and extensive travels, Franklin likely experienced one of the fullest lives ever lived. The truest of American patriots, he would doubtless take issue with the towering size and poor results of today's Federal Government. "*Well done is better than well said,*" he wrote nearly 300 years ago.[39]

---

[39] Poor Richard's Almanack, 1737.

To keep the promise of the U.S. Constitution, well-functioning government is not an option. Yet, due to a long history of manufactured complexity, what the Federal Government accomplishes in 1,000 steps could be done in 10 or 1, or maybe none. With complexity, inefficiency is assured, as is thievery. Spending is pushed higher – not to accomplish more but just to keep pace with diminishing returns. We don't need to drill down into budgets to see the problem; Washington's bottom line tells it all. The AU professors' formula for making problems bigger is Washington protocol. Politicians gleefully ride the spending wave. It's their ticket to leveraging the Federal Government's enormous wealth to reward donors and get re-elected.

With every misstep there's an explanation. Congressional inquiries and the Office of the Inspector General (OIG) investigations show how the Federal Government is willing to admit mistakes, while demonstrating no willingness to correct them. They shine a bright light on problems, reporting what was learned, and leaving it at that. There is no Office of Follow Through and Completion (OFT&C) in the Federal Government. Rather, Washington is a confederation of never-ending loose ends. Far removed from the source of needs, the Federal Government is out of touch and years behind.

With every promise to do better, Washington introduces another layer of bureaucracy to observe, analyze, and report. Operating costs increase, but results remain on the same downward path. Putting hammer to nail is not a skill of the Federal Government; neither is moving in increments. Its footprint is too big to be nimble: think "hippo doing ballet." When a toothpick is needed, Washington furnishes a two-by-four.

The continuous handing down of law, regulation, code, ruling, policy, executive order, and the amendments that follow add unnecessarily to everyday hardships. One example we're all familiar with is U.S. tax code, formally known as the Internal Revenue Code (IRC).

The Taxpayer Advocate Service (TAS) is an independent organization of the Internal Revenue Service (IRS). In their 2008 Annual Report to Congress, in a section labeled "*Most Serious Problems,*" TAS highlights the "*Complexity of Tax Code*" and reports that in 2006 the cost of compliance was "*$193 billion – or a staggering 14 percent of aggregate income tax receipts.*" In TAS's 2012 Annual Report to Congress, the complexity of tax code is again highlighted under Most Serious Problems. Many of the arguments made in the 2008 report are repeated in 2012, including this one: "*If tax compliance were an industry, it would be one of the largest in the United States.*"

Both reports point out the staggering size of the tax code, writing, "*the Code has grown so long that it has become challenging even to figure out how long it is.*"[40] In 2012, TAS solves this mystery: "*using the 'word count' feature in Microsoft Word turned up nearly four million words.*"[41] In published form, U.S. Tax Code is 9 feet wide. It's so big and complex that not a single tax accountant in the U.S. knows it all.

In a follow-up to the TAS report, Congress did the usual and held a hearing. Under the title of "*Protecting Taxpayers From Incompetent And Unethical Return Preparers,*" the hearing was convened April 8, 2014, one week before the annual tax return deadline. Despite the fact that they are the body guilty of keeping tax code complex, it was an opportunity for Congress to feign concern for the burden they themselves impose on the country. Among the witnesses called was National Taxpayer Advocate Nina Olson. As in

---

[40] Taxpayer Advocate Service — 2008 Annual Report to Congress — Volume One. Page 4.

[41] Taxpayer Advocate Service — 2012 Annual Report to Congress — Volume One. Page 6.

the TAS reports from 2008 and 2012, where she's cited, Olson explained, *"Because the tax code is so complex, the significant majority of taxpayers pay preparers to complete their returns for them. Unfortunately, many taxpayers have no easy way to determine whether the preparer they are hiring can do the job."*

For two and a half hours, the Senate Committee on Finance heard from a wide range of witnesses, including Ms. Olson. However, as we've come to expect, nothing changed. Change is not in the interest of Congress. Many of their constituencies and donors profit from the intricacies of U.S. taxes. Besides, taking on a project like streamlining tax code is too much work and, even worse, outside the political spotlight. True to form, since the 2014 hearing, Congress has added to the tax code but done nothing to simplify it. In their 2020 Annual Report to Congress, the National Taxpayer Advocate once again cites among its Most Serious Problems the *"[b]arriers to tax law compliance, including cost, time, and burden."*

A lot of our time and money goes into playing along in Washington's game of manufactured overhead. The country swims against an upstream current of inefficiency created by Congress and the Federal bureaucracy. Other than to raise revenues to fund the government, the *"process"* of paying taxes has no inherent value.

For this reason, our goal should always be to make tax compliance simple. When we drive down the cost of tax compliance the willingness to pay increases. This is what Europe has observed. In many countries, tax obligations are presented online in *"pre-completed"* form, and in as few as one or two pages. The taxpayer can accept or dispute the pre-completed report. Most do the former and carry on with their day. Time and money saved; stress spared. This approach has been widely used in the Nordics. Perhaps it explains why

Finland, Denmark, Sweden, and Norway rank at the top of the world's happiest countries.[42]

In the U.S., we have moved in the opposite direction. From 400 pages in 1913 (when federal taxes were introduced) to 73,954 pages as of 2013[43]. According to a Tax Foundation report published in 2016, tax code is "*almost six times as long as it was in 1955 and almost twice as long as in 1985.*"[44] While the commoner wallows in an ocean of regulation, those who are better off benefit. If you're part of the $193 billion industry that provides tax services, a long and complicated tax code is your friend. It keeps you busy and helps you find new and creative ways to save money for rich clients.

Nothing is wrong with providing tax services or saving money. The problem is that we're rewarding the wrong behavior. Our focus is not on being a more productive nation but rather a busier one. This isn't capitalism but the corruption of it. Describing the Protestant ethics that spur capitalism, Max Weber wrote in 1905, "*Waste of time is the first and in principle the deadliest of sins.*"[45]

What we witness in the complexity of tax code has its markings everywhere in the Federal Government. Even when presented with an opportunity for efficiency and simplicity, Washington finds it impossible to break from the past. From the bank crisis of 2007 to the COVID pandemic of 2020, the Federal Government will argue that it needed to step in and act. This may be true, but why don't budgets drop when the country is not in

---

[42] The World Happiness Report is a publication of the United Nations Sustainable Development Solutions Network.

[43] A Short History of Government Taxing and Spending in the United States, by Michael Schuyler. Tax Foundation. February 19, 2014.

[44] The Compliance Costs of IRS Regulations. Scott A. Hodge. June 15, 2016

[45] "The Protestant Ethic and the Spirit of Capitalism." By Max Weber. 1905

crisis? Is the threat faced in World War II a never-ending one today, or have we simply given up on running the Federal Government efficiently?

Despite a workforce of about 62,000 and an Information Technology Services budget of $1.9 billion, the Social Security Administration struggles.[46] While the onslaught of retiring baby boomers and inaction by Congress are not helping, SSA inefficiencies add to the cost of government. As the biggest part of the entire U.S. budget, at $1.2 trillion for fiscal year 2021, the SSA's website downtime mentioned earlier is indicative of a government adrift.

The compound effect of our aging population and inefficiencies in Washington will require an estimated 23% reduction in Social Security payments by 2034.[47] Given Congress's cash burn rate, we shouldn't be surprised if this estimate is off by years.[48]

Another example of the Federal Government's hierarchy of uncultivated excess is the Office of the Inspector General (OIG). The OIG identifies fraud, waste, abuse, embezzlement, and the mismanagement of people and funds. Congress created the first Inspector General (IG) position in the Army in 1777, but it wasn't until the Inspector General Act of 1978 that the OIG's role in the Federal Government was solidified. Starting with 12 offices, the OIG has since grown to 74.[49] With the passage of the Inspector General Reform Act of 2008, the Council of the Inspectors General on Integrity and Efficiency (CIGIE) was formed.

---

[46] FY 2021 Congressional Justification
[47] "3 Sad Facts About Social Security" by Sean Williams. The Motley Fool. February 10, 2018.
[48] In 2017, the Social Security Board of Trustees projected that by 2022 payments going out will exceed revenues coming in.
[49] Inspector General Vacancy Tracker. Pogo.org. February 11, 2021.

Oversight.gov, created by CIGIE, is the public database of Inspector General reports. It's also a report card on OIG's overall progress. On its homepage (screenshot below) are three charts: *potential savings; reports uploaded, and recommendations made.*[50] For fiscal year 2021: potential savings equaled "$62.7B"; total reports uploaded "18,994; and recommendations made numbered "5.23K" [51]

Through its offices, the OIG acts on reports of fraud and other illegal activities in defense of the Federal Government's budget. With the continuous raid by unscrupulous contractors on Washington, the role of the OIG is essential. However, as the actual money saved and recovered is so small, the OIG cunningly focuses on *potential* savings and not *real* savings. Under the banner of *Integrity and Efficiency,* the OIG shows us Washington's impulse to pretend. So far removed from the real world, effectiveness is not measured by what *was* done but rather by what *could* have been done. Imagine if you withdrew money from your bank account not based on its actual balance, but instead based on what that balance could be. Imagine a publicly traded company announcing earnings based on potential, and not actual, profits. Insane, but this is how the OIG does its accounting.

---

[50] Full titles of sections: "Potential Savings Identified in Reports on this Site;" "Number of IG Recommendations in Reports on this Site;" and "Reports uploaded to Oversight.gov." There are 9 types of reports, ranging from Investigation to Disaster Recovery. https://www.oversight.gov/

[51] 18,994 is the total of all reports uploaded as of mid-February 2021.

As seen in the OPM and OMB workforce report, mentioned in the previous chapter, nothing in the Federal Government lives outside the illusion of action. A closer look at Oversight.gov shows Washington's escalating overhead and inefficiency. During Oversight.gov's first decade (1990-1999) 341 reports were uploaded. During the past decade (2010-2019) that number has gone to 14,977, an increase of 44 times.[52]

On the surface, this jump would seem to indicate that the fraud perpetrated by Halliburton in Iraq has become commonplace. While this may be true, the real explanation is Washington's incessant need to leave no stone unturned, regardless of cost, as if in a frantic search for the holy grail of governmental utopia. The OIG's approach would work in a system that is responsive to recommendations and seeks improvements. But this is not the case in Washington where spending rules.

Washington's tachometer is pointing to red; the engine is revving at max RPMs, but the transmission is stuck in neutral.

Key to the production of waste is the ability to offer recommendations yet remain detached from putting those recommendations into practice. Of the thousands made by the OIG, the overwhelming majority were never implemented. As with Healthcare.gov, the real value of the OIG to taxpayers can be measured in fractions of pennies. Searches on Oversight.gov for *performance, results, or outcomes* reveals thousands of reports. However, upon reading these reports, we learn that what are being seen as *performance gains* are measured in checklists completed and reports written. While these may be steps in the right direction, the fact is that very few OIG recommendations ever see the light of

---

[52] From the OIG's first report, their Semiannual Report to Congress, issued April 27, 1990, through the end of 2019 the number that decade to December 31, 1999, a total of 341 reports were uploaded. Searching ahead ten years, from January 1, 2000, to December 31, 2009, a total of 689 reports were uploaded. However, over the next decade, from January 1, 2010, to December 31, 2019, uploads jump to 14,977.

day. Tangible results are hard to find and, invariably, packaged in wording that's hard to decipher.

In 2020, in its semiannual report to Congress, the Office of Inspector General for the Department of Labor (DOL) shows "*Monetary Accomplishments*" of $74.8 million.[53] On first reading this the impression is that stolen money and/or property was recovered. However, a review of the report's appendices tells us this isn't the case and that the figures given are highly inflated.

Of the $74.8 million in Monetary Accomplishments, the biggest portion, $34.7 million, is attributed to what the OIG calls "*Recoveries.*" This is defined as "*the dollar amount/value of an agency's action to recover or to reprogram funds or to make other adjustments.*" In other words, the $34.7 million that OIG sites as "recovered" is another estimate of potential savings and not an actual record of it. The OIG also assigns a value to "*Cost-Efficiencies*" and awards itself a monetary accomplishment of $21.6 million based on "*management's commitment*" to "*utilize the government's resources more efficiently.*" Seventy-five percent of what's being reported as "*Monetary Accomplishment*" is based on optimistic assumptions and not results. In "*Restitutions/Forfeitures, Fines/Penalties, and Civil Monetary Actions,*" the DOL's Office of the Inspector General recovers $18.4 million. But that's only one-fourth of the $74.8 million savings stated in the DOL report. Not what you'd expect from a team that touts *Integrity and Efficiency.*

---

[53] Semiannual Report to Congress Office of Inspector General for the U.S. Department of Labor Volume 84, (April 1–September 30, 2020)

In the report's appendices we see the extent of the Federal Government's problem. The issue is not that the OIG recommendations are bad but rather that nobody seems to have the capacity, or will, to implement them. An entire section of the appendices, 9 pages in total, is dedicated to "*Unimplemented recommendations.*" Regrettably, there's no page for "*Implemented recommendations.*"

Unlike most governments, the U.S. Federal Government is generous with its data. Starting with the Freedom of Information Act of 1967, Washington has maintained a tradition of openness. Reports that can be hard to get in most countries are available online and free of charge in the U.S. Websites like USAspending.gov and Oversight.gov provide many valuable insights and are a source of Federal Government assets. But, as noted in the OIG's report, these assets are potential and not real. Essentially, they're sitting on the bookshelf alongside thousands of other potentials, all waiting to be acted upon but backed up indefinitely by a system that doesn't differentiate between sizzle and steak. As we'll see in the next chapter, these problems are remedied in a bottom-up approach where resources are aligned with need and where recommendations are put forward at a pace consistent with the ability to implement them.

Among the many OIG reports are some particularly noteworthy ones: "Learning from Iraq" and the previously mentioned "Overview Of 60 Contracts" on the Healthcare.gov implementation. Both make clear that the Federal Government is incompetent in managing money, people, and projects. On Iraq, the OIG writes: "*What was concluded painted a very grim picture of our ability to adequately plan, execute and oversee large-scale stability and reconstruction operations.*"[54] On Healthcare.gov, the OIG writes: "*We found*

---

[54] Learning From Iraq: A Final Report From The Special Inspector General For Iraq Reconstruction. July 9, 2013.

that HHS and CMS made many missteps throughout development and implementation that led to the poor launch of Healthcare.gov."[55]

Stated in their own words, the trend is clear: the Federal Government lacks planning, execution, oversight, and implementation skills. In other words, of the key talents required to complete a project successfully, the Federal Government has none.

Why then do we entrust Washington with trillions?

Size

One-hundred-forty-eight is a special number according to British anthropologist Robin Dunbar. It's the limit of meaningful relationships we can manage. Once relationships grow beyond 148, they become *"unstable and begin to fragment."*[56] The number of neocortical neurons in our brain limits *"information-processing capacity"* and this, says Dunbar, *"limits the number of relationships that an individual can monitor simultaneously."*[57]

Despite the brain's amazing capacity, we have limited bandwidth on the matter of meaningful human interactions. It's a limit many companies recognize and work within. Beyond 148 employees, inefficiencies emerge, objectives grow fuzzy, and waste multiplies. It's no wonder that small teams are much more productive (and generally better workplaces) than big teams. In fact, beyond Dunbar's limit a big team is really not a team

---

[55] "An Overview Of 60 Contracts That Contributed To The Development And Operation Of The Federal Marketplace." August 2014. Daniel R. Levinson. Bolded font added.

[56] "Neocortex size as a constraint on group size in primates" R.I.M. Dunbar Journal of Human Evolution. June 1992. Publisher: Elsevier

[57] ditto

at all. Now, imagine working in the Pentagon where just the *"management team"* consists of over 26,000 people. Despite the fog of never-ending confusion, things get done there too. But, on average, it's at a cost hundreds or even thousands of times what it should be. This markup is not the result of any improvement in our defense, but rather the cost we pay when we allow inefficiency to thrive.

This doesn't mean that large organizations don't succeed. Many do. The difference is that those organizations streamline for efficiency and build teams within the 148 limit. One well-known example is W.L. Gore & Associates, the creators of Gore-Tex. When their team sizes exceeded this limit, they built additional office space. *"Creating these defined ecosystems allowed individual buildings to keep their sense of association. A sense of solidarity rises when recognizable faces are working as a unit toward similar objectives."*[58]

While his landmark research is specific to group size, Dunbar's findings are reflected in our inability to grasp the intricacies of law and tax code. These, too, have grown beyond human limits. What could once be answered by an individual now takes a committee. There are no email alerts. Silently, we go from understanding something *well* to understanding it *somewhat* to being *overwhelmed*. It's the *Hierarchy of Competence* in reverse.[59] Our numbers are fuzzy because our vision is blurred.

As of 2021, the Department of Defense website reports a headcount of 2.9 million *"Service Members & Civilians."*[60] In the OPM and OMB *Federal Workforce* report, cited earlier, the rest of the Federal Government is about 2.1 million. However, the OPM/OMB report didn't include 16 agencies estimated to make up over 710,000 employees, including

---

[58] Solving Dunbar's Number by Dylan Ramirez. Sift. July 19, 2016

[59] Hierarchy of Competence: Unconsciously incompetent; consciously incompetent; competent; unconsciously competent.

[60] https://www.defense.gov/our-story/

500,000 from the U.S. Postal Service, an *"independent agency"* of the Federal Government. Altogether the actual size of Washington's non-defense bureaucracy is 2.8 million people.

Combining the 2.9 million in defense agencies with the 2.8 million in civilian agencies, we see a Federal Government made up of 5.7 million employees. (That's *two-and-a-half* times the size of Walmart's 2.2 million, the U.S.'s largest workforce.) Add in an estimated 4.1 million contractors, and the actual size of the Federal Government swells to 9.8 million people.[61]

Efficiently managing an organization that numbers in the millions is impossible even with the best managerial team. Factor in the intrigues of politics, and it's no surprise that Washington's return to the taxpayer is at or approaching zero.

Until 1933, when the New Deal was launched, most of the Federal Government resided in the Eisenhower Executive Office Building (EEOB).[62] A majestic building adjacent to the White House, it was originally named the State, War, and Navy Building. At the EEOB the U.S. was *"formulating and conducting the nation's foreign policy in the last quarter of the nineteenth century and the first quarter of the twentieth century — the period when the United States emerged as an international power."*[63] What were once offices for the entire Federal Government – during some of the country's most productive years – is now home to a *"majority of offices for White House staff."*[64]

---

[61] "The True Size of Government," October 2017. New York University Professor Paul C. Light put the Government's size at 9.1 million, as of 2015.

[62] Also, the site of my motorcycle accident as a messenger in 1976.

[63] Eisenhower Executive Office Building. White House Website. https://www.whitehouse.gov/about-the-white-house/the-grounds/eisenhower-executive-office-building/

[64] Eisenhower Executive Office Building. White House Website. https://www.whitehouse.gov/about-the-white-house/the-grounds/eisenhower-executive-office-building/

The Federal Government's size is mind-boggling, literally, as evidenced by the inability of OPM and OMB to give a precise answer to the question on headcount. How many people actually work for the Federal Government remains a mystery. Theoretically, these problems could be ignored were it not for Washington's out-of-control spending and worsening underperformance. While budgets and national debt have been a subject of debate throughout U.S. history, it wasn't until about twenty years ago that things turned noticeably worse.

The difference between what the Federal Government collects in taxes (receipts) and what the Federal Government spends (outlays) determines a budget surplus or deficit. Adding all past deficits together is how we calculate today's debt. As defined in Investopedia: "*The national debt is simply the net accumulation of the federal government's annual budget deficits.*"[65]

Since the dawning of operational America in 1789, and for 210 years through the end of the twentieth century to 1999, the debt was $5.6 trillion.[66] During this period, the Federal Government ran at a loss most years, but that loss was relatively small compared to what it is today. Remarkably, in its first sixty years, from 1789 to 1849, the Federal Government ran a surplus of $70 million.[67] The country had paid off its Revolutionary War debts and was moving forward. Small and unencumbered by the legacy of laws and tax code we face today, the Federal Government in those early years was able to get on with the business of governing. Whether they knew it or not, their management style was lean.

---

[65] The National Debt Explained

[66] Table 1.1—Summary of Receipts, Outlays, and Surpluses or Deficits (-): 1789–2025. White House. Office of Management and Budget. Historical Tables https://www.whitehouse.gov/omb/historical-tables/

[67] US federal budget receipts and outlays : Actual and estimates 1789-2019. US Government Printing Office and BEA - US Bureau of Economic Analysis. (https://stats.areppim.com/stats/stats_usxbudget_history.htm)

From 1998 to 2001, the Federal Government proved that it could run at a surplus. Economic tailwinds helped, but it was a clear sign that the U.S. – private and public sectors alike – were doing the right thing. Then came September 11, 2001, and prosperity took a backseat to fear. Not only were innocents lost that terrible day, but a nation was too as evidenced by the skyrocketing debt that followed, summarized in the following table.

Period (years)	Deficits	Average	Explanation
2002 – 2006 (5)	$2.6 trillion	$.539 trillion	Wars: Afghanistan & Iraq
2007 – 2011 (5)	$6.2 trillion	$1.256 trillion	The Great Recession
2012 – 2016 (5)	$4.7 trillion	$.956 trillion	Slow Recession Recovery
2017-2019 (3)	$3.1 trillion	$1.048 trillion	Operational Inefficiency [68]
2020 – 2021 (2)	$5.7 trillion	$2.854 trillion	Covid Pandemic
TOTAL (20)	$22.3 trillion	$1.115 trillion	

Source: U.S. Treasury

Over the past twenty years we have, on average, added $1.115 trillion to the debt every year. This is how we went from a debt of $5.6 trillion in our first two hundred years to over $30 trillion during the past twenty. From 1950 to 1999, the average annual deficit increase was $107 billion. From 2002 to 2021 this average increased by over 10 times, while the total debt quadrupled.

No longer just a downward trend, Washington is now on a collision course with our national debt and its uncertain consequences. Our politicians – preoccupied with re-election – may have forgotten the warning of Founding Father John Adams, who said: "*There are two ways to conquer and enslave a nation. One is by the sword. The other is by debt.*"

---

[68] From 2017 – 2019 economic growth averaged 2.5%

When Federal Government spending goes from 20% of the country's GDP to 30%, as it has in recent years, the impact is enormous. Like it or not, the Federal Government ends up controlling more of the economy and, therefore, more lives and livelihoods. Were Washington acting with the competence of the Finnish Government, there would be little room to complain. However, because of Washington's enormous size and wasteful practices, the opposite is true. The more ingrained the Federal Government is in the economy, the more our losses compound. The tug-of-war over ideologies played out in Washington is Congress's reflex reaction to distract the country from the harsh realities of the nation's balance sheet.

In its mismanagement of the country's finances, Congress turned what was originally a good idea, the debt ceiling, into a blank check on America. Compensating for its inability to deliver results, what started as a Coca-Cola to give the Federal Government a lift every now and then has now become a cocaine addiction. The cost of our dependency in 2021 was an interest payment of $562 billion ($562,000,000,000). Half a trillion dollars, just on interest! As the debt grows, so does the hole we find ourselves in. Unless we change course, every year a bigger and bigger part of taxpayer money will be consumed by interest payments on the country's debt.

Not only must the U.S. taxpayer shoulder the Federal Government's debt, but it's also the U.S. taxpayer who's underwriting that debt. The social security and disability Trust Funds that save for millions of Americans is the largest holder of U.S. Treasury bonds, worth $2.9 trillion as of 2020.[69] The governments of Japan and China are the second and third largest holders of Treasury's bonds at $1.3 trillion and $1.1 trillion, respectively.

---

[69] The Old-Age and Survivors Insurance (OASI) and Disability Insurance (DI) Trust Funds

Since the beginning of Social Security in 1935, what was collected in taxes and not paid out was put into safe U.S. Treasury bonds. Historically, this arrangement was a good one. Annual interest payments added nicely to the Funds surplus. Unfortunately, the demographics of 2022 are not the demographics of 1935. In recent years, these funds have been dishing out more than they're taking in. The Board of Trustees for Social Security and Medicare has been warning about this for some time. In their annual 2020 report, they repeat their concern in the report's summary: *"Social Security and Medicare both face long-term financing shortfalls under currently scheduled benefits and financing."*[70]

While on the hook for the country's debt, the taxpayer is also on the hook as its prime lender. If Congress stops raising the debt ceiling, Treasury will default, and Social Security will collapse. This is the worst-case scenario and not likely to occur anytime soon. However, what we do know is that social security payments are forecasted to decline by 2035. As the Board of Trustees explains: *"At that time, the combined funds' reserves will become depleted and continuing tax income will be sufficient to pay 79 percent of scheduled benefits."*[71] This drop in Social Security will push millions of Americans into poverty. We should do everything in our power to reverse it.

It's a rare occasion when anything is simplified in Washington. But simplify is what Congress has done on the matter of the debt ceiling. Raising it is not so much debated as assumed. Essentially, once a budget passes Congress without the money to fund it, the debt ceiling automatically increases to fill the gap.[72] Debt production is Washington's default setting.

---

[70] "A SUMMARY OF THE 2020 ANNUAL REPORTS" by Social Security and Medicare Boards of Trustees https://www.ssa.gov/oact/trsum/
[71] Ditto. An earlier reference "3 Sad Facts About Social Security" by Sean Williams. The Motley Fool. February 10, 2018. Puts the drop at 23% or 77% coverage.
[72] H.Res.6 — 116th Congress (2019-2020) reinstated the Gephardt Rule.

For many economists, the issue is not so much debt, as its ratio to GDP. Looked at historically, the U.S.'s debt to the GDP ratio first exceeded 100% from 1945 to 1947, averaging 112%. Concerning as that may have been, it was justified considering the wars being waged against Germany and Japan. Both posed an existential threat to the U.S. and its allies.

Following the Second World War, for sixty-years (1948 to 2008), the debt-to-GDP ratio averaged 52%. However, as shown by the Federal Government's DATALAB (usaspending.gov), in 2009 it breached 80%. From 2010 to 2012 the ratio of debt to GDP increased to 91%, 95%, and 99%, respectively. From 2013 to 2019, it exceeded 100% every year, averaging 103%. For 2020, the debt-to-GDP ratio reached 130%.

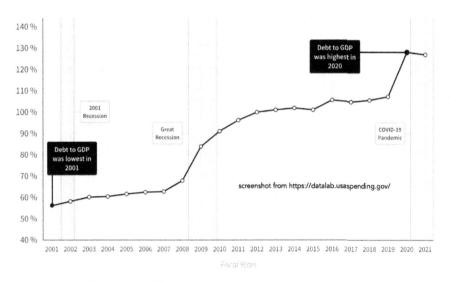

Source: Usaspending.gov DATALAB

Some point to Japan's debt-to-GDP ratio, at over 250%, as proof that concerns about the U.S. debt are exaggerated, especially as central banks work to keep interest rates low. But Japan's debt trend only emerged in the 1990s. It's hardly a reliable economic metric to follow. Furthermore, the Yen is not the world reserve currency that the U.S. Dollar is. Japan doesn't have to worry about losing a privilege it doesn't have.

Despite this, the issue that should concern us more than mounting debt is mounting inefficiency, running at high speed. Two-hundred and thirty-three (233) years of laws, codes, and processes that are a mangled patchwork of their original versions. This is the core problem; debt is a symptom of it.

Even when it tries to bypass its own bureaucracy, Washington slams up against shortcomings of the very system it created. Direct payment is the most effective way of distributing money to individuals and organizations. But because of the Federal Government's outdated methods and tools, billions are lost in the process. A 2013 U.S. Treasury strategic objective states: "*The federal government currently operates under multiple financial systems and accounting practices, leading in some cases to challenges in communication and coordination.*"[73] By "*challenges,*" Treasury is referring to the billions of dollars lost and stolen due to "*communications and coordination*" problems.

A February 2021 update to the CARES Act is more specific about the extent of Washington's failure. The Inspector General for the Department of Labor (DOL-OIG) reports that the "*improper payment estimate*" for its Unemployment Insurance (UI) program "*has been above 10 percent for 14 of the last 17 years.*"[74] With consumer credit

---

[73] "Improve the efficiency and transparency of federal financial management and government-wide accounting." 2013.
Performance.gov Defunct webpage: [obamaadministration.archives.performance.gov/content/improve-efficiency-and-transparency-federal-financial-management-and-government-wide.html#progressupdate. Bold font added.

[74] "DOL-OIG Oversight of the Unemployment Insurance Program." February 3, 2021.
https://www.oig.dol.gov/doloiguioversightwork.htm

card fraud considerably lower than the fraud perpetrated against Washington, one must wonder why the Federal Government is guardian to the country's finances.[75]

Washington leaks billions, knowingly, and does nothing more than report the bad news. In the same report cited above, DOL-OIG writes: *"At least $63 billion of the estimated $630 billion in UI program funds could be paid improperly, with a significant portion attributable to fraud."*

For years to come, we'll be hearing about defrauders being brought to justice. They should be, but the Federal Government's cost and overhead of doing so will only result in a net loss for the country. More parading of justice under the law, but at a significant cost to America's bottom line. The average American is distracted from such matters. We're simply too busy making a living and entertaining ourselves. This shortcoming is capitalized on by elected officials who grandstand efforts to crack down on fraudsters without mention or consideration of the costs involved in doing so.

The best way to avoid the cost of prosecution is to limit the necessity for it. But this is not the Washington way. Fixing things requires work; politicking takes a lot less effort. Responsible for trillions of dollars and billions of transactions, the U.S. Treasury needs to be several steps ahead of fraudsters. By their own admission, they're several steps behind. A sitting duck for those lurking in the shadows with bad intentions during desperate times. Billions are looted by scammers who have been studying the Federal Government's weaknesses for years. Washington knows this, has been reporting about it for years, but is unable to act.

---

[75] Card Fraud Worldwide 2010-2027. 2019 The Nilson Report. 6.8 cents on the dollar as of 2020.

Tethered to the distant past and bogged down by its massive bureaucratic bulk, the U.S. Federal Government is incapable of managing and dispersing funds with minimal loss. This problem is only made worse by months of political wrangling and non-stop feuding, followed by a mad rush to shovel money out the door when legislation is finally, and dramatically, passed.

Nothing has been done to address the ongoing losses identified by the Treasury, but Congress did give us DATA (the Digital Accountability and Transparency Act) and with it USAspending.gov; our around-the-clock update on how much money Washington is fire-hosing away. In its DATALAB, we see the Federal Government's daily burn rate. From an average of $11.5 billion a day in 2013, to $13.7 billion a day in 2019 and $18.9 billion a day in 2020. Compared to 2013 these increases represent jumps of 20 and 65 percent, respectively. Increases of this size are not just a reflection of the country's stress due to COVID but more evidence of dysfunctional government.

The DATALAB numbers are a call to action. They show a nation in the process of being stripped naked. There is no deep state or evil actor behind this demise. The Federal Government money problem will not be fixed by outing a politician or nuking a party. It's a systemic problem that must be addressed systemically.

For the most part, the Federal Government's bureaucrats are blameless. The majority work in an academic setting. The use of words like *efficient* and *lean* are part of internal training programs and Black Belt certifications, but not practiced to the level required to have any impact.[76] High-level civil servants and agency secretaries with the best plans fail.

---

[76] Black Belt Certification. "Local commands graduate 12 trained to lead innovation" Aug. 26, 2019. Naval Sea Command Systems.

Not because their plans are no good, but because of the undertow of the Federal Government's dysfunctionality – a sort of riptide that sucks people and missions into the deep blue sea of oblivion. To say this riptide is draining the economy and the country is no longer an exaggeration. That reality grows by the day.

To remain competitive on the world stage, and with China, our focus must be on producing value, not throwing money at yesterday's problems. China doesn't care about our politics or debt. They have a plan of their own and are acting on it. As a single-party state, they can move decisively and quickly. There is debate, but it's limited and not in the public forum.

In the U.S., it's the opposite. Decisions are hard to decipher, take too long to make, and cost too much. This doesn't mean abandoning the values of our democratic republic but instead recognizing the need for profound change if we're going to maintain one. Despite its messiness, when it works, democratic consensus triumphs over single-party dictates. Always.

The media industry is another Washington parasite, pretending to educate a nation but only taking it further into the deep weeds of Federal Government excess. Real news is fixed in duration, but opinions about that news can go on for hours, days, and weeks. The longer discussed and analyzed, the greater the revenues. Media glamorizes Congressional crazies and robs the nation of its ability to think and reason by manufacturing opinions for its viewers. Arousing shock and despair works wonders in creating a following.

We argue over ideologies and turn to misinformation and conspiracies because they're easier to onboard, particularly if they harmonize with our views. This is not a problem of party affiliation but one of human nature. Under stress, we fall into the trap of putting *"negativity and escape before positivity and approach,"* to quote Daniel Kahneman.[77] Pragmatism, once the country's greatest virtue, no longer has a place at the table in Washington.

The situation we find ourselves in is no one's blame, nor should it be. Blaming offers no value to the country. We've argued enough. We need to leave finger-pointing to the past and act like the advanced nation we are. If we don't, we'll have to learn to adjust to life in a lesser world. The bright shining light of opportunity will dim and, for many, go out. That's happening already. The signs are in front of us.

Continuing on this path doesn't end America but takes it from a first-world country, and a place of democracy's success, to a second-rate nation where liberty takes a back seat to survival. The consequences of the U.S.'s demise will rattle all democracies and upset world order. What we're experiencing now are tremors, growing stronger by the day.

Politics

Like spraying gas on a fire, today's political environment works as an accelerant when combined with the Federal Government's ailments of age, complexity, and size. Addressing the effects of these ailments is reserved for Congressional hearings, campaign speeches, and primetime interviews. Resolving them is another matter and not appealing in a fundraising-centric political system that puts swagger before solutions.

Article I Section 8 of the U.S. Constitution defines the responsibilities of Congress. Nowhere in Section 8 is campaign fundraising mentioned. Fundraising is, however,

---

[77] Thinking, Fast and Slow. Daniel Kahneman. Page 300 "… *negativity and escape dominate positivity and approach.*"

priority #1 for members of Congress, particularly for those who have ambitions of pleasing party bosses and being re-elected. Section 8 does instruct Congress to *"pay the debts"* and provide for the *"general welfare"* of the United States. But in today's Washington, taking on issues like Treasury's 2013 strategic objective to save billions of dollars for taxpayers is politically unattractive. It takes time, requires a lot of work, and is hidden from public view and donors: the exact opposite of what a politician needs to be re-elected.

Upon arriving at the Capitol and taking an oath to uphold the Constitution, the first thing members of Congress do is break it. Like a newlywed slipping out the backdoor to meet a lover, our elected officials slither down the street from the Capitol to party headquarters to raise money. Protective of its sacred institution, members of Congress, Democrat and Republican alike, are not allowed to raise money from the Capitol. The guilt of violating an oath is lessened when separated from where that oath was taken.

On April 24, 2016, the 60 Minutes report *"Dialing for Dollars"* reveals the extent of money's impact on Congressional behavior. In detail, House Representative David Jolly explains how members of Congress are given calls scripts and issued quotas. Jolly's was $18,000 a day. *"You never see a committee working through lunch because those are your fundraising times,"* Jolly says. Hoping to curtail this practice, he introduced the STOP Act (H.R.4443) in February 2016. With tepid support, the STOP Act was dead on arrival. Jolly lost re-election later that year.

Rather than applying the Federal Government's assets to serve the country, Congress's workday revolves around raising money for one's party and re-election. No longer performed just in the build-up to an election, fundraising is a never-ending job in Washington. Driven by money and living in the bubble of an open-ended debt ceiling, Congress is motivated to squander, not spare. Considering the billions now invested in political campaigns, this should come as no surprise.[78] Senators and House Representatives are obliged, first and foremost, to compensate their supporters. Should they forget, there are armies of lobbyists to remind them.

Many in that army were previously in Congress. The Center for Responsive Politics lists 477 that made the journey from politician to lobbyist.[79] No longer champions of the American people, these former politicians instead apply their inside knowledge to benefit corporations, special interests, and themselves.

One wonders about the resources expended by politicians while in office to achieve a position of favor with wealthy lobbies. Given the reality of losing re-election, an exit strategy would seem like a must-have for any politician. Landing a plum position as a lobbyist is not a bad outcome and perhaps even a goal sought by some upon arriving in Washington. In the maze of hard and soft money outlets in the Federal Government, there are many avenues for compensating donors.[80] Having been on the inside, a former politician-turned-lobbyist knows how to navigate this maze. It's not illegal. It's simply how money and power flow in the halls of Congress.

In 2003, Google CEO Eric Schmidt said: *"There were 5 Exabytes of information created between the dawn of civilization through 2003, but that much information is now created every 2 days."*[81] Our capacity for attention is fixed, yet the information pushed at us skyrockets. Treasures are revealed but so are demons. According to *Attention Economics*,

---

[78] Funding for the 2020 races for the White House and Congress are estimated at over $14 billion. Twice the spending of 2016.

[79] Revolving Door Summary. Center for Responsive Politics. OpenSecrets.org. May 1, 2021. https://www.opensecrets.org/revolving/top.php?display=Z

[80] Hard money outlets = contracts to donors. Soft money outlets = legislation, tax breaks, etc., to benefit donors.

[81] An exabytes is a 1 followed by 18 zeros (1,000,000,000,000,000,000).

attention is a scarce commodity. In the whiplash of American politics, that scarcity is exploited.

In today's environment of bitter and divisive politics there is no regard for the 9th Commandment: *thou shalt not bear false witness.* Personal attacks pressed and repeated become fact whether true or false, and regardless of how they may degrade or endanger others. Even for devout Christians, lying about one's opponent is no longer a sin but justified, ironically, in the name of God. Bitter and divisive politics has been the norm for ages. The problem today is that it runs algorithmically, faster than thought, and beyond human control. It is created, shared, updated, and repeated at a pace that demands more than the human race can offer.

Adding a touch of hysteria to a campaign is emerging as perhaps the most effective tactic for advancing one's name. The recipe is simple. Take a contentious issue, sprinkle it with disinformation, then imagine it in the extreme. Suddenly, a molehill looks like a mountain in the two-dimensional world of love and hate. If an opposing candidate wins, gloom and doom are sure to follow. It's not true, of course, but treated as a certainty. Logic, turned inside-out, is sure to grab attention and bring in campaign donations. Political rhetoric, magnified by the media, takes us from being better informed and thoughtful to reactive and angry. We support positions that we often don't understand but are ready to die for. As the complexities of the tax code rob the country of time and money, a media that embraces mania denies the country of dialogue. Reporters chasing politicians isn't what it appears. They're both players in the same game.

In the beginning, campaigning didn't exist in the United States. Self-promotion and fundraising were considered uncouth, particularly for the affluent. Our first six presidents – Washington, Adams, Jefferson, Madison, Monroe, and John Quincy Adams – were well off and well-connected. It wasn't until a relative commoner, Andrew Jackson, ran for office that campaigning first appeared. Jackson had lost to John Quincy Adams in 1824 and was determined to achieve a better outcome in 1828. He succeeded by recruiting supporters to distribute his campaign pamphlets. Jackson didn't engage in any fundraising, but he did reward some supporters with positions in his administration.

In 1828 the tug-of-war between campaigning and corruption officially kicked off in the American political system. Seventy-two years later, in 1905, while looking at ties between insurance companies and Wall Street, New York investigators noticed something unusual. Insurance companies had been making significant contributions to political campaigns in 1896, 1900, and 1904. Despite benefiting from those contributions in winning the presidency in 1904 (though denying any knowledge of them), President Theodore Roosevelt called for a ban on corporate donations. In his 1907 State of the Union Address, he urged Congress to curb corruption and improve transparency to "*hamper an unscrupulous man of unlimited means from buying his way into office.*"

Later that year, Roosevelt signed the Tillman Act. It was a first attempt at regulating the flow of money to power and, simultaneously, a challenge to unscrupulous men to find new ways of carrying out old tricks. While shaming some, transparency emboldened others. Awareness may educate and enlighten, but it can also anger and alienate.

With all the commotion surrounding politics, we're left with the impression that keeping one's seat in Congress is highly competitive. It isn't. The retention rate for members of Congress is over 90%, twice the retention rate of CEOs, CFOs, and other C-level positions in corporate America. A trend toward a less competitive Congress was first observed in 1974 by Yale professor of Political Science David Mayhew. In his paper,

"*Congressional Elections: The Case of the Vanishing Marginals,*" Mayhew observed that from 1956-72 "*the number of districts with close House elections dropped precipitously.*"[82]

The cause for this drop wasn't clear to Mayhew in 1974. Today we know why it happens. Money flows to those in power and not to those challenging power. Incumbents are better funded than new candidates because the incumbent is more likely to win. If you represent a business or special interest, your money is safer with an incumbent than a challenger. It's not that bets are never placed on challengers; it's just that our risk-averse nature makes us more inclined to bet on a past winner than a future one. Money doesn't just corrupt politics, it defeats it. As ideas, dialog, and debate stagnate, a political system rots.

Money, media, and mania rolled together produce the frenzy that characterizes Congress. We all hate it, but oddly we can't seem to get enough of it. Better than reality TV, Congressional drama runs $24x7x365^3$ (cubed). We pay to see it, we pay to produce it, and we pay when we're seduced by it.

In today's politics, informing a constituency is not as effective as scaring it. Dazed in a world of information overload and attention deficits, nothing draws one's focus better than bad news. Studies in behavioral economics show that we're two to three times more likely to respond to bad news than good news. Known as *risk aversion*, its effect in politics, where passions run hot, is likely even more pronounced. In risk-averse politics, our first and often only thought is centered on the worst of people. Fears are locked and loaded behind a wall of hate that's impenetrable and blind. Reasoning is reduced to pre-recorded answers. Reaction comes quickly and without thought. This is not a problem of political

---

[82] Mayhew, David R. 1974. "Congressional Elections: The Case of the Vanishing Marginals." Polity. 6:295-317.

affiliation – Democrat or Republican or Independent – but one of pushing up against the limits of human engineering.

From Banker to Customer: Losing World Currency

At an internal Oracle Corporation gathering outside Washington in 1990, an economist spoke. On the topic of the national debt, which totaled $3.2 trillion at that time, the economist had an interesting outlook. *"If you owe the bank $1 million,"* he said, *"you're a customer. If you owe the bank $1 billion, you're the bank."*

I wonder if the economist would hold the same outlook today, with U.S. debt over $30 trillion. Over eight times what it was in 1990, just thirty years ago.[83]

In Washington's fundraising-centric world, age, complexity, and size go from benign tumors to malignant ones. Money's influence motivates Congress to undermine the very system it has promised to protect. As a result, the *"general welfare"* of the United States, stipulated in Article I Section 8 of the Constitution, is subverted by a political system where winning comes at all costs.

Ninety-five percent of the world's population lives outside the U.S. Most neither understand nor care about Democratic or Republican politics. What they know is what they see: political turmoil, social instability, and skyrocketing debt. All behaviors that undermine U.S. creditworthiness and the confidence of those holding U.S. debt.

---

[83] As of the end of Fiscal Year 2020 on Sept. 30, 2020, the federal debt was $26.9 trillion and the debt to GDP ratio for FY 2020 was 129%.

As the American dream dims for some, others see opportunity. In the crosshairs is the world reserve currency. In 1944 the U.S. Dollar (USD) was established as the world reserve currency. As Europe stood in shambles, America shone. Since then, with borrowing cheap and easy, the U.S. has had what France's Finance Minister and later President, Giscard d'Estaing, described as an "*exorbitant privilege.*"[84] In a fundraising-centric political system, that privilege works against us. Political agendas, not actual needs, drive budgets. Trillions are spent, yet many of the country's biggest problems, from infrastructure to education, remain in disrepair. We may think of this as strictly a domestic matter, but as the U.S. political system wages a civil war and mindlessly drives up debt, the world watches.

Debts should, eventually, yield a tangible return. Amazon ran up debt for years, but they were creating long-term value in the process. There is merit to modern monetary theory (MMT) which posits that high public debt-to-GDP ratios are acceptable if the debt is for resources that create long-term benefit. However, the combination of money's influence on politics and the Federal Government's overwhelming inefficiencies prevents long-term benefits. Congress has entombed the U.S. in a sinkhole of debt whose horrors will unravel as the privilege of world reserve currency slips away.

It will be painful. Interest rates on the dollar will jump, and payments on the debt will increase by hundreds of billions. As of 2021, the U.S. debt interest payment was $562 billion.[85] In a world without the privilege of the world reserve currency, interest payments could quickly exceed $1 trillion. The financial hangover will be hardest on retirees and

---

[84] "*Exorbitant privilege*" was how Finance Minister Giscard d'Estaing described the U.S. Dollar advantage in the 1960s. He would later serve as President of France (1974 – 1981).

[85] $562,388,232,682.17 - U.S. Department of the Treasury Bureau of the Fiscal Service. TreasuryDirect. https://www.treasurydirect.gov/govt/reports/ir/ir_expense.htm.

the disabled. The Social Security cuts forecasted for 2035 will come sooner and go deeper. Such is the harsh reality when one goes from banker to customer, and with a pile of debt.

Europe is no longer the U.S. ally it once was. While economic ties remain strong, political, and strategic relationships have changed. In the past, European leaders skillfully adjusted to U.S. presidents of both parties to maintain an alliance that has stood since the Second World War. That tradition ended in 2017 under the America First agenda. It came as a shock to European leaders to see their long-established playbook with the U.S. discarded. Reluctantly, Europe recognized it was on its own. Future U.S. administrations may attempt to turn back the clock, but the fear of losing that alliance again remains fixed in the European mind. Europe will not wait for a second chance at America First.

The threat posed by Russia weighs more heavily on European leaders today than at any time since 1961, when the Berlin Wall was erected. As Putin embarks on a reckless campaign of expansion into Ukraine, Europe grows increasingly anxious. An alternative to the protection Europe long enjoyed from the U.S. is required. The best, and perhaps only, answer is China. China shares a 2,699-mile border with Russia, has a military budget four times the size of Russia's, and a population nearly ten times bigger. Even during their glorious Sino-Soviet days, friction between China and Russia almost came to war in 1969.[86] Much stronger today than in 1969, no country scares Russia more than China. While Putin bullies European and NATO leaders, the opposite is true of China's President Xi Jinping. In the presence of Xi, Putin bows.

---

[86] Sino-Soviet border conflict in 1969. Lasted seven months. Causalities: China 248; Russia 58.

On December 30, 2020, China and the EU took a significant step in strengthening their ties. They agreed, in principle, on a Comprehensive Agreement on Investment (CAI).[87] EU concerns about human rights, and China's reaction to those concerns, have stalled the CAI. Behind the scenes, it's likely negotiations continue. Aside from its impact on U.S. trade, an EU-China agreement will advance a goal shared by both: to replace the USD as the dominant world reserve currency.[88] The America First agenda called for a transactional relationship, and Europe is playing along, not out of spite but necessity.

Trading volume is one of the key determinates of world reserve currency status. As of 2020, China is the EU's biggest trading partner of goods. Imports and exports total $673 billion. The EU – U.S. trade of goods is slightly lower at $638 billion. However, the services trade between the EU and the U.S. is five times the EU's services trade with China: $490 billion versus $98 billion. Altogether, the EU trades over $1.1 trillion in goods and services with the U.S. and $770 billion with China.[89] In addition, the EU trade balance is negative $184 billion with China and positive $149 billion with the U.S.

From an economic perspective, it would seem that the EU should remain loyal to the U.S. and the USD. However, being risk-averse like the rest of humanity, European fears of Russia take priority over a favorable trade balance with the U.S. If Ukraine slides under Russian control, others could follow and imperil the EU. In the wake of a fractured U.S. partnership, an EU-China strategic alliance would do much to soothe European fears vis-a-vis Russia. It also provides momentum for edging the USD off its reserve currency perch and replacing it with the EURO (or Renminbi).

---

[87] EU-China Comprehensive Agreement on Investment. December 30, 2020. European Commission. https://bit.ly/2SPu2eYd

[88] "Towards a stronger international role of the euro." European Commission contribution to the European Council and the Euro Summit. 5 December 2018

[89] Figures are from European Commission for 2020 (goods) and 2019 (services).

As of 2019, China was the world's largest exporter at $2.6 trillion, slightly ahead of the U.S.'s $2.5 trillion.[90] The EU ranked third with $2.4 trillion in world exports.[91] Combined, exports from China and the EU total $5 trillion, that's 26% of world exports, and twice U.S. exports.[92] If the EU can keep itself together, Europe, aided by the tailwinds of reserve currency status, will emerge as the financial crossroads between the U.S., China, and the rest of the world.

Most economists will argue that the likelihood of the EURO or Renminbi replacing the USD is slim. Both the EU and China face growing debt and have large bureaucracies, too. However, unlike the U.S., China and the EU are relatively young governments. China's one-party system came to power on October 1, 1949, and the European Union's start began on November 1, 1993. Neither is saddled with the 233 years of laws, tax codes, and complexities that burden the U.S. And neither has a Congress that exploits those burdens for political gain.

For years we've heard that China will surpass the U.S. as the world's next superpower. Congress and the Federal Government's performance only hasten this eventuality, not just by heaping on debt but also by acting in ways that undermine American assets and the integrity of the American brand. Losing the privilege of dominant reserve currency will not be the end of the U.S., but it will undoubtedly mark the beginning of our fall from power. When the U.S. can least afford it, the country will be hit by a tsunami of its compounded waste and ineptitude. Restoring reserve currency status and the American brand will, at a minimum, take decades.

---

[90] International Trade Centre

[91] Export of goods from the EU 2010-2020.

[92] Statista. "Trade: export value worldwide 1950-2020." By Tugba Sabanoglu, May 7, 2021. https://bit.ly/3grcy1G

233 years is a remarkable run for any government. Now, the unimaginable is upon us. Our central government is sinking and taking the country with it. We can let it pull us under, or we can act exceptionally, do the hard thing, and re-align Washington with the country.

Revolution is an ugly thing and has many unintended consequences. We can do better in the modern age because we know better. As we saw in Intel's 90-degree turn to the Pentium chip, a company was redefined. In the end, Intel not only developed a superior chip, but they also identified a new way of computing and a roadmap to their future. They didn't throw the baby out with the bathwater but instead pivoted to a new and radical approach. It wasn't in Intel's nature to make this change, but they soberly read the facts in front of them and responded intelligently. They took on a monumental challenge and succeeded.

Despite not being the leading microchip manufacturer today that it was when the Pentium was introduced in 1993, thousands of companies have followed in Intel's path and pivoted from the edge of disaster to success. The United States of America can do the same by remaking its democratic republic and returning government to its essential job of solving the needs of the country, and at a reasonable cost.

3 THE PIVOT

"Town meetings are to liberty what primary schools are to science; they bring it within the people's reach, they teach men how to use and how to enjoy it."

Democracy in America Alexis de Tocqueville (1835)

The Concept

The 90-Degree Turn is a political theory meant to redefine the role of central democratic governments in general and the U.S. Federal Government in particular. Its name is borrowed from the Intel story told in the Preface. It should not be taken literally, as some aspects of the 90-Degree Turn are more of a 180-degree turn, or no turn at all. I had to give a name to the theory and choose this one.

Despite its name, the objective of the theory is to create a process for pivoting Washington from a cash-burning, politically charged operation to one that provides tangible solutions (i.e., value) at a reasonable cost. The goal is not just to make the Federal Government efficient but also to make it relevant. Relevant means addressing today's problems – not based on an ideological agenda, but instead on the country's locally-validated needs.

We must abandon 233 years of bureaucratic strata, and a political system skilled at exploiting that stratum, to get to this point. This is not accomplished by dissing or demolishing Washington but instead by re-aligning its bureaucracy and its legislative body, Congress, with the country.

Re-aligning Washington

The 90-Degree Turn begins by making Washington responsive to the country it's destined to serve. Rather than the traditional top-down approach, this theory flows in the opposite direction, from the bottom up. At its core is a national survey that functions as a *Needs Monitor* for the country. The survey – available to all Americans – organizes needs by town, city, county, state, region, and country. The Needs Monitor functions as a virtual townhall meeting and a platform for local and state governments to collect, curate, organize, share, and submit their requirements to Washington.

Rather than Washington issuing an RFP to solicit goods or services that it thinks are needed by the country, local governments will issue RFPs to Washington. Rather than Washington expending resources (money and people) on things the country may not need, resources are instead allocated according to locally validated needs. As the *Needs Monitor* is shared throughout the country, political leaders and citizens alike learn what issues are most pressing in different parts of the country, and the country as a whole. This approach offers a chance to team with others, find answers, scale solutions, and drive down costs. Through this bottom-up process, we determine which parts of the Federal Government are essential, which are redundant, which should be repurposed, and which should be let go.

Aligning needs with resources that create solutions is where the rubber meets the road. Politicians will be held to account for adherence to, or departure from, the stated needs of citizens and the RFPs produced by local government. Here political gimmickry is crippled, if not crushed.

National Survey

As well as a practical method for transforming the Federal Government, a national survey that tracks and measures local wants, needs, and solutions can neutralize our national divide by removing us from the blinding anger that dominates politics today. By focusing on local needs – the ones we're most familiar with and that most impact us individually – the country can break from debating the obtuse abstractions of Washington politics and get back to the business of America. In this bottom-up workflow, where local needs intersect with the assets of Washington bureaucracy, we have a good fit. Where intersects don't exist or are redundant, we have an opportunity to cut or repurpose resources, with an emphasis on the latter. The aim is to transform Washington, not to ruin careers or the economy.

Neither the tools nor willingness for a national survey existed in 1787 during the drafting of the Constitution. United in their determination to create a nation, the Founding Fathers were not united in their outlook on the average citizen. In the opinion of many, the commoner was not knowledgeable enough to vote. One exception was Dr. Benjamin Franklin, who, at the ripe age of 81, had the experience to know the shortcomings of great men and the resourcefulness of commoners.

In 1787, sixty percent of the U.S.'s three million citizens could read. Today, that percentage is ninety-eight, and the population is over one hundred times bigger. A commoner in the 21st century consumes more knowledge in a week than would have been available in a lifetime during the 18th century. We may consider our neighbor an idiot, but he's vastly more knowledgeable than his doppelganger idiot from 1787.

With an informed population, the need for top-heavy Federal government evaporates. This might explain the show put on by Washington politicians (perhaps unconsciously), to distract the nation from their on-going record of failures. The demands of fundraising-centric politics drown out the voices of common citizens and common sense. By tuning out Washington noise and focusing instead on local needs, the Federal government can begin to provide value again.

This challenge is made all the greater by a media industry that thrives off politics and is incentivized to create alarm. The media understands the lure of loss-aversion and knows it will draw more eyeballs, and revenue, by reporting on contentious issues rather than helping to build bridges. In the new millennium, news is no longer delivered at set morning and evening intervals, as it was fifty years ago, but rather non-stop on TV, phone, and the web. The volume of news and social media content is more than the human brain can process. Our attention limits are fixed and don't expand with the inflow of more information. The hyperbolic rise in media content, from CNN to TikTok, doesn't inform us as much as it undermines our ability to think. As attention wanes under the weight of information, answers eclipse insights. This is the reality distortion field that's a product of a vast media industry. We're too well informed to listen and too sure to question. Opinions are not formulated but presented as fact. We've become a nation with an attention deficiency disorder.

The media, and social media, are largely to blame, but we must admit our complicity in allowing them to become such a big part of our lives. Some who recognize this problem have heeded the advice of Cal Newport, author of _Digital Minimalism: Choosing a Focused_

Life in a Noisy World. Most of us, however, are too distracted to read his book and apply its principles.[93]

The sheer volume and repetitiveness of news is mind-numbing. Media drains us of time while filling us with anger. A return to the 1960s when Walter Cronkite reported the news, and Eric Sevareid commented on it, would be a wonder.[94] Everything we needed to know was eloquently delivered in 30 minutes. We were free to interpret what we heard and debate it around the kitchen table. Our time wasn't spent listening to the opinions of others as much as formulating our own. It was a time prior to CNN, when we didn't feel the need to be the first to know.

We can't deny content traveling at the speed of light any more than we can deny free speech. Despite this, we should recognize that while data may be the new oil, *information-overflow*, a byproduct of mass media, is a chronic condition that impacts our ability to think and act rationally.[95] If speech is truly a freedom, we should put limits on it and protect it with guardrails. In its current run-away form, it does more harm than good.

De-centralized D.C.

When invited to the Constitution Convention in 1787, Patrick Henry, a staunch supporter of state rights who feared a dominant federal government, said, "*I smell a rat.*" His senses were acute. Today we see the rat.

---

[93] *Digital Minimalism: Choosing a Focused Life in a Noisy World. By Cal Newport. Published 2019.*

[94] Walter Cronkite (November 4, 1916 – July 17, 2009) was an American broadcast journalist who served as anchorman for the CBS Evening News for 19 years (1962–1981). Eric Sevareid (November 26, 1912 – July 9, 1992) was an American author and CBS news journalist from 1939 to 1977. Source: Wikipedia

Wikipedia. "Information overload (also known as **infobesity, infoxication, information anxiety, and information explosion**) is the difficulty in understanding an issue and effectively making decisions when one has too much information (TMI) about that issue, and is generally associated with the excessive quantity of daily information."

Our founders were primarily citizen politicians. As farmers and local merchants, they were attuned to their constituencies. They usually had established professions before becoming political leaders. Today's leadership, on the other hand, is dominated by professional politicians who often spend most of their careers in the Federal government and, understandably, are less attuned to local needs.

If Washington was attracting individuals like those who drafted the Constitution, there would be less need for concern. But the opposite is true. As turnover in politicians drops, leadership wanes, and lunacy flourishes. Politicians have become a separate class; outrage is their currency, transported via the world wide web and propelled by its effectiveness at fundraising. Unfortunately, solutions and fundraising clash. Those who promote solutions find themselves out of office. They either fail to get reelected – often eliminated in primaries by doctrinaires from their own party – or they leave out of frustration with getting anything done. Many of Washington's best have left.

To win at reelection finger-pointing, half-truths and lies are easier than problem-solving. Politicians have learned how to arouse the electorate, attract money into their campaigns, and distract the country from their grotesque spending addiction. With the Federal Government outlays now accounting for one-third of the entire U.S. economy, we can all safely say: "*We are government.*"

A lot has changed in 233 years since the U.S. Federal Government went into operation. Technological advancement that was barely noticeable during the nation's first century has been head-spinning during the past century. While its ideological foundation remains as sound today as when the Constitution was signed in 1787, the tripartite checks and balances constructed to fulfill the Constitution's promise have been undermined by two dominant political parties that permeate all branches of government.

A fundamental re-making of politics and government's bureaucracy are needed to put Washington on the right path. The 90-Degree Turn is conceived as the means for making this a reality by de-centralizing Washington's bureaucracy and binding its future to the productive, and cost-efficient, use of its assets. As a bottom-up process, budgets are made and managed locally. Rather than the White House's Office of Management and Budget (OMB) formulating a budget for the entire country, state governments will formulate budgets to include their needs for Federal Government assets. Given the financial limits they continuously breach, terminating Congress's control of money is the most pressing near-term issue facing the country. State governments may fail, but those failures are localized and relatively small compared to Washington's.

This approach serves as a critical step in pivoting from a bulky Federal bureaucracy to a lean de-centralized one. Rather than pushing demands on the country – and spending wildly in the process – the role of the Federal Government will shift to applying its assets to address the needs of state and local governments. This bottom-up process forms the sieve that separates the essential elements of the Federal Government from everything else.

In healthcare, *translational medicine* refers to the implementation of proven methods to treat and prevent disease. Lifesaving research often never sees the light of day. Translational medicine, referred to as *"bench to bedside,"* is intended to correct this. We might think of the 90-Degree Turn as translational government, from *"agency to action."* As healthcare is inherently more complex, translational government should be easier to achieve, assuming we have the will to make it happen.

What about defense, space, national security, foreign services, and other national priorities in the 90-Degree Turn? They're not eliminated, of course, but instead placed alongside local priorities. On matters of national defense, it will be the role of the Department of Defense to make its case. But, rather than in Congress, the vote on the appropriation of defense spending will happen locally.

For example, if the Pentagon determines that the country should build a new generation of stealth bombers, it will need to sell its plan to the country, not Congress. In this way, local governments can compare the cost and benefits of other priorities (e.g., healthcare, housing, water management, infra-structure) to their portion of a stealth bomber initiative. While backroom dealings will never disappear entirely, the possibility of donors bagging billion-dollar contracts – that the country knows little about – will be difficult in this setting. Like the transformation of Federal Government assets, defense and national security decisions will be decided and funded from the bottom up. Certainly, classified matters like stealth bombers and spy satellites cannot be shared in the public forum. However, funding decisions in support of such projects can be. In the final analysis the goal is to restore common sense and proportionality to budgeting decisions.

Won't state and local governments act in their own interests on national matters? Of course, that's to be expected and, perhaps, encouraged. State and local government should serve their local constituencies first and the country second. However, as history has consistently shown, where a national emergency exists, Americans are ready to band together. Despite politics, religion, or race, it's in our nature to help one another, particularly in times of crisis. This is a truth that pre-dates the Constitution and, I would argue, an exceptional aspect of the American character. *E pluribus unum.*

Will state government perform better than Washington? Most state governments are hindered by bureaucracy that, like Washington's, is excessive, inefficient, out of touch, and threatened by corruption. A bottom-up Needs Monitor will benefit states in the same way that it benefits Washington. By separating assets from overhead, redundancy, and waste, state government can streamline too. We may achieve better control over spending by taking that responsibility away from Congress but fall short of tangible results if state and local governments are not participating. We should aim for both. State and federal governments should act as one in addressing the needs of the country.

As a nation made up of 50 states, the U.S. has an inherent advantage: it's already decentralized and well suited to implement a bottom-up model. Rather than blue and red states, our focus shifts to how well states are performing in addressing the needs of their citizens. Cities in China compete with one another based on objectives decided in Beijing. Unlike China's top-down model, a *Needs Monitor* assesses performance from the bottom-up. Towns, cities, counties, states, and regions in the U.S. could compete based on the validated needs of their citizenry. Comparisons made on the news networks too often focus on the cost of housing, taxes, and job opportunities. But there are hundreds of other aspects of a community that can make it a great place to live or, maybe, a place to avoid. By enabling everyday Americans to be heard in a structured and organized way, we can reassess and recalibrate the country's direction. As that guidance is not coming from Washington, *we the people* need to find it ourselves. We have the knowledge and technology to make this happen.

Congressional Clean-up

Despite the Treasury's stark 2013 warning of *"communication and coordination"* problems that were robbing the country of billions (and perhaps trillions), Congress did nothing.[96] Doing so would have interfered with spending, and that could jeopardize reelection.

---

[96] 2013 U.S. Treasury strategic objective titled "Improve the efficiency and transparency of federal financial management and government-wide accounting"

Rather than stopping to repair a smoking engine, Congress puts pedal to metal, rolling the dice on America's future. What was initially a persistent leak of money is now a torrent of fraud and waste, adding to the country's debt, and gambling with the lives of millions.

Article I of the U.S. Constitution outlines the responsibilities of Congress. Section 8, of Article I, defines Congress's role concerning the collection and management of money. Its first paragraph reads: "*The Congress shall have power to lay and collect taxes, duties, imposts and excises, to pay the debts and provide for the common defense and general welfare of the United States.*"

Those who drafted the Constitution didn't think it necessary to advise Congress to act with reason and common sense. Having to spell this out would have been ungentlemanly in 1787, like speaking to an adult as though he were a child. Psychology, as a science, didn't exist in their day, but the Founders knew the evils of money, particularly in the hands of the insecure. Despite this, as campaign fundraising didn't exist in their day, the Founders were blind to a future they couldn't imagine.

Given our mounting debt and the Federal Government's dismal results, it would seem clear that Congress is not meeting its obligation under the Constitution to provide for the "*general welfare*" of the United States. Instead, Congress has become a source of mass psychosis that distracts the country from taking note of its abysmal performance. Rather than acting on Treasury's 2013 strategic objective to save the country billions, Congress has only added to our burdens by manufacturing more complexity.

Against this backdrop, the role of Congress in the 90-Degree Turn pivots away from legislating new laws and tax codes, to curating, updating, and simplifying the ones we already have. It's not an easy project but must be done to return the country to a productive future. As those solely responsible for creating law and tax code under Section I of the Constitution, the buck for streamlining both stops with Congress.

In the 90-Degree Turn, Congress's primary role moves from debating and legislating to curating and simplifying. Rather than adding to the country's immeasurable mountain of laws and 9-foot-long tax code, Congress will be tasked with a bottom-up process of its own. Like the bottom-up method described previously for identifying assets in the Federal Government's bureaucracy, Congress's focus will turn to identifying the Federal Government's most important legal and tax code assets. This means assessing local needs and ensuring that laws and code work in support of those needs.

Law is the backbone of a just society and a sound economy. However, when laws and tax code multiply, complexity follows. Costs rise, and trust falls. Lawyers and tax advisors benefit, but there's no value to the country. Today, we live in a world of Government manufactured overhead whose cost is a burden to every American, including lawyers and accountants. The 90-Degree Turn changes this. If the priorities for local government are water management, healthcare, housing, and infrastructure, then these areas should be priorities for legal review and simplification. Given the Library of Congress revelation that it's "*nearly impossible*" to know how many laws we have, it doesn't make sense to focus on *all* laws and tax codes but only on the relevant ones.[97]

It's an oversimplification to think that removing complexity from law or tax code will work in all cases. Complex scenarios often necessitate complex solutions. Despite this, our goal in lessening the burden of law and tax code on the country is to strive for relevance

---

[97] Frequent Reference Question: How Many Federal Laws Are There? March 12, 2013, by Jeanine Cali. https://blogs.loc.gov/law/2013/03/frequent-reference-question-how-many-federal-laws-are-there/

and simplicity. We will not succeed In all cases, but to significantly improve, we don't have to.

From Heavy-Handed to Helpful

Washington has an all-or-nothing approach. It's why they fail at so many things and why nothing happens in a measured way. As we saw in the invasion of Iraq and the development of Healthcare.gov, Washington instinctively throws bushels of money at problems.

In stark contrast, in a *lean* world, even large and sophisticated projects start with small teams and build as needed over time. This is the exact opposite of what we saw in the development of Healthcare.gov, the world's most expensive website that kicked off with 60 contractors and, to date, has cost the taxpayer over $2 billion (about 200 times what it should). In the lean mindset, we learn what's needed, build (or provide) a solution to address that need, and then measure its effectiveness. *Lean* is an ongoing process designed to shed waste, fine-tune performance, and deliver results. Widely proven in established and startup businesses, lean management provides a framework for Washington to pivot from heavy-handed to helpful.

In the 90-Degree Turn, Congress is responsible for chartering a new set of laws for the United States of America. Their goal is to transform law from the arcane and challenging to the understandable and ordinary. In the process, Congress is guided by relevance, clarity, simplicity, and the ability to write (or revise) laws so that citizens understand them.

In the 90-Degree Turn, members of Congress will abandon their history of top-down lawmaking. Instead, they will focus on streamlining existing law with an emphasis on cutting out the extraneous and complex. In the process, they will seek to replace mandates with *nudges*. Laws, like tax code, are a means to an end. Their value is measured by the degree to which they uphold our convictions of justice, liberty, and prosperity. As laws and tax codes grow big and convoluted, they interfere with these principles.

The Lawmakers

While lawyers may be good at making laws, they are not the insightful judges of human nature they may believe themselves to be. Few are trained in data analysis or psychology. One exception is Cass Sunstein, an expert in law and behavioral economics. In his book, Simpler: The Future of Government, Sunstein describes his experience in Washington at the OIRA (Office of Information and Regulatory Affairs). He writes: "*We closely monitored the number and the cost of rules, and when we declined to proceed, it was often to reduce cumulative burdens and to ensure against undue complexity in the system... We recognized that when high costs are imposed on the private sector, it is not only some abstraction called 'business' that pays the bill. Consumers may pay too ...*"

Offering a new outlook on law, Sunstein looks at the social environment in which laws are made. In this context, he introduces us to the *Nudge*, the title of another book he wrote, this one with Richard Thaler.[98] Unlike many legal experts, Sunstein understands that regulation is most effective when it leads (nudges) people in the right direction without telling them where to go. Sunstein explains that "*good nudges should be taken as a crucial part of simplification.*" Measurable for their effectiveness, the "*best nudges,*" writes Sunstein, "*have high benefits and low costs.*"

Cass Sunstein understands that less is more. He offers a tested model for guiding Congress in its quest to charter a new set of laws for the country. His approach furnishes a template

---

[98] Richard Thaler is the renowned Professor of Behavioral Science and Economics at the University of Chicago, who coined the term "behavioral economic."

for making laws user friendly, less intrusive, less costly, and ultimately more effective. Using Sunstein's approach, the temptation for legal overreach is countered by looking for the best nudge. It's on Sunstein's chopping block of *choice architecture* that Congress can begin its cleanup, perhaps with a Cass Sunstein at the helm.[99]

While it may be to the displeasure of politicians, the pivoting of Congress is the most essential part of this theory. The reason, quite simply, is that Congress is not only dysfunctional but dishonest. It is a body that has been the source of festering madness throughout history, starting with the Roman Senate. Given too much power and the wrong incentives, elected officials begin behaving more like mad hatters than distinguished members of a country's legislative body. We shouldn't abolish Congress, but rather turn it upside down and give it a new purpose within the framework of Article I.

With simpler laws and tax codes, confidence is restored. People are more willing to play by the rules when they understand them. As noted by both the U.S. Taxpayer Advocate and the European Union, simplicity makes for clarity and results in a higher percentage of the population paying their taxes.[100]

States versus Federal

Following the Revolutionary War, the newly founded United States of America was in a state of revolt. While France, Spain, and the Netherlands pushed to be paid for the loans they'd made (crucial to winning the Revolution), merchants in Europe and America

---

[99] Choice architecture is the design of different ways in which choices can be presented to consumers, and the impact of that presentation on consumer decision-making.

[100] A) U.S." The most serious problem facing taxpayers — and the IRS — is the complexity of the Internal Revenue Code (the "tax code")." The Complexity of the Tax Code Taxpayer Advocate Service — 2012 Annual Report to Congress — Volume One. B) EUROPE "Fair and Simple Taxation: Commission proposes new package of measures to contribute to Europe's recovery and growth." European Commission Press Release 15 July 2020

demanded payment on bills long past due. Caught in the middle were Revolutionary War veterans who had not been paid promised wages and faced heavy taxes and the prospect of foreclosure on their homes and farms.

In October 1781, as Massachusetts artillery officer Lieutenant Colonel Ebenezer Stevens prepared for the Revolutionary War's final battle in Yorktown, Virginia, problems were surfacing back home. The trigger that threatened to topple Massachusetts occurred on October 4 of that year, when a Groton constable "*took a pair [of] oxen from Capt. Sheple....*"[101] Sheple's claim that he had "*lost his livelihood*" became a rallying cry for others, including Groton town Selectman Job Shattuck.[102]

A former British soldier turned American patriot, Shattuck had fought at Bunker Hill and Saratoga. Now, along with eighteen others, he participated in the "Groton Riots," the name given to a series of attempts to obstruct tax collectors and push back on the Commonwealth's aggressive tactics to pay off its large war debt. A successful farmer, Shattuck owned the most property in Groton. Despite this, with British ports closed to American goods, the economy took a nosedive. This made matters difficult for all farmers, including the successful ones.

Without the funds to support a federal military, no action would be taken against Shattuck until years later. In the meantime, the pressure to pay taxes did not abate and citizen pleas to address grievances went unheeded. Within a few years of the Groton Riots, more aggressive efforts were mounted by Daniel Shays, Luke Day, Eli Parsons, and hundreds of others in central Massachusetts. They blocked courts from addressing debt

---

[101] October 4, 1781, entry in William Nutting's Diary, Massachusetts Historical Society.

[102] "The Groton Riots of 1781" by Gary Shattuck. Journal of the American Revolution. May 29, 2014.

cases and attempted to overtake the federal arsenal in Springfield. The revolution that had driven out the British was now a revolution to take back Massachusetts.

Designed with a weak central government in mind (to avoid a repeat of the oppression experienced under British rule), the Articles of Confederation proved inadequate for America's future. This inadequacy was quickly exposed when the weak central government was unable to settle foreign debts or compensate veterans of the Revolutionary War. Failure to meet financial obligations caused riots, disrupted trade, and resulted in economic decline. More authority needed to be allocated to a central government if the newly founded United States of America was to reach its full potential. With the country's thirteen states operating as separate entities, our collective power was negated. The Constitution resolved this by giving Congress the power to regulate foreign and interstate commerce, create a national court system, and establish an executive branch to enforce the law.

The pendulum of power that had given little sway to the central government under the Articles of Confederation now swung in the opposite direction. A stronger federal government was a necessary move that gave the United States the ability to act as one economic entity.

It all made sense in 1787 and was the right thing to do, as evidenced by the country's success since. However, the equilibrium sought between state and federal government has, over 233 years, gravitated toward the center. Today, Washington's unabated influence on power and money resembles a magnet, pulling in everything within its force field and growing more imbalanced by the minute. The process that created Washington in 1787 needs to be put in reverse.

Washington has a spending and inefficiency addiction that is pushing the country to the brink. The fastest and most logical way of addressing this addiction is to remove Congress from its control over spending. We no longer have the time for incremental steps. State governments face challenges and shortcomings of their own. Many of these resemble what we witness in Washington. Despite this, it's necessary to remove the U.S. Congress from its control over budgets and spending, and to delegate this responsibility to state governments. This doesn't mean that the many essential functions of central government such as interstate commerce, foreign trade, and defense go away, but simply that the control of money in support of these is managed locally by the 50 states.

In the upward flow of the *Needs Monitor,* towns, cities, counties, and states can avail themselves of an opportunity to align with their citizenry. They too can focus on validated needs and refine their bureaucracies by pivoting from process to purpose, while adopting lean management principles and employing nudges over mandates. Some may fear that too much control in the hands of local and state governments will undermine constitutional safeguards that protect all Americans. These safeguards include justice, tranquility, liberty, and our general welfare. However, pivoting from a dysfunctional Congress to an efficient one doesn't undermine these principles but rather breathes new life into them.

The rise of China

As China rises, there is fear. Despite sometimes embarrassing displays of its imperfections and a recent history of reckless wars, American democracy is widely preferred over China's single-party authoritarian state. However, as government's sole purpose is to improve the wellbeing of its people, there is little doubt that Beijing, in the past 50 years, has outperformed Washington As Washington falls behind, democracy weakens – not just in America but around the world. Against this backdrop, authoritarianism flourishes.

To counter China's rise, Washington must demonstrate value. This starts by measuring *benefits provided* versus *dollars spent*.

Americans believe that freedom, tempered by the rule of law, is the best way to create a happy and thriving society. Public debate and argumentation, while sometimes discomforting, are the catalysts that lead to advancement. America's success is proof that nobody has all the answers and that societies work best when everyone has a chance to participate. That's democracy, at least in principle. Messy, perhaps, but ultimately offering greater value and a future that is a distant dream for most under authoritarian rule.

The problem is that freedom – including the freedom to advance – is impeded when order decays. This is what Goethe meant when he famously said he preferred injustice to disorder.[103] Washington's old age, mounting complexities, and massive size undermined order. Add to this the venom of fundraising-centric politics and it's easy to see why Congress has failed and will continue to fail.

Today, we don't participate in Washington as much as Washington participates in us. More like reality TV than a gathering of responsible adults, Washington, aided by media, has put the country into a spin. There's no one to blame other than those who recognize this problem and fail to act. This includes *we the people*. By severing the flow of money to the Federal Government we not only restore order and accountability to the country, but

---

[103] I would rather commit an injustice than endure disorder. (Ich will lieber eine Ungerechtigkeit begehen, als Unordnung zu ertragen.) 1787

we also disrupt the intoxicating tango of Washington fundraising-centric politics and the media. Substantially fewer *breaking news* reports out of Washington will provide oxygen to a nation short of breath and put the country on a course that eventually surpasses China.

THE IMPLEMENTATION

Whether you believe you can do a thing or not, you are right.
Henry Ford

The Theory and Practice of Creating Value

I t would be incomplete, and maybe unfair, to put forward a theory without getting into the details of how to implement it. Every last turn, twist, and permutation will not be worked out. Doing so goes against the grain of keeping things simple, streamlined, and relevant. What we do want, however, is an understanding of the core concepts of the 90-Degree Turn. Not to formulate answers but, firstly, to re-imagine government.

The celebrated 17th century French mathematician and philosopher, Rene Descartes, wrote: *Cogito, ergo sum.* I think, therefore I am. From Descartes' perspective, the essence of being was *thinking* and *self-awareness*. In the 90-Degree Turn, the essence of being is *doing* and *creating value*. Value represents boots on the ground in the struggle for better government. While remaking Washington and statehouses, through value we redefine how democratic republics operate in the 21st century.

Value equates to meaningful solutions that make life better. Cars provide value in enabling us to move freely about, and GPS provides value in helping us to move about more efficiently. Value is found in quality education and healthcare. Value – unlike most of what Washington produces – is tethered to real needs, produced at a reasonable cost, and delivered in a timely manner.

Value, combined with democratic principles, is our best tool for elevating humanity and containing tyranny – foreign and domestic. It's also our highest hope for world peace.

Value is not a government report sitting on a desk piled high with similar works. In the 90-Degree Turn, theory and practice go hand-in-hand. We begin with an objective and work backwards. Known as goal-seeking, it's the opposite of the Federal Government's institutional top-down outlook that often has no purpose other than to empty a budget or make a political statement.

In the 90-Degree Turn, money is not spent on what *might* be needed but only on what *is* needed, based on locally defined requirements. In today's Washington, potential needs are not differentiated from actual ones. This happens in a world where the biggest sin one can commit is not spending their entire budget. I encountered this when selling to the Federal Government.

One incident stands out. It happened during my time with Alliant Computer. There was a project in the Pentagon's Accounting Office that involved building a new computer facility to house many of the latest and fastest computers on the market. The project was well underway when I learned of it and saw the project manager's blueprint. It included an Alliant and computers from many of our competitors. I imagined a quick sale with little work.

Unfortunately, my enthusiasm was quickly dashed when I asked about the nature of the problem the DoD project manager hoped to address. His answer was to see how well scientific computers could be used to speed up office applications for word processing and spreadsheets. Nobody in the real world, or the Pentagon, encountered issues with office applications that required scientific computing. But as there was money to be spent, the Pentagon's Accounting Office went in search of a solution for a problem that didn't exist. Eventually, the project was recognized as ridiculous and shut down, but only after millions of dollars had been wasted.

Where needs are defined locally and aligned with state and federal government from the bottom up, costly adventures like the DoD's Account Office project never see the light of day.

Similarly, rather than another Inspector General report to nowhere, funds are not allocated where there's no plan for action. Government should not be a sandbox for all things possible, but instead a place where resources are aligned with needs for the purpose of creating value. Those who cheat government and taxpayers alike should be held accountable. However, when the cost of finding and prosecuting scammers exceeds the gain, we shouldn't bother. The lesson is to make government accountable and not a beehive of litigation to uphold the principle that stealing is wrong. Besides, when pleas from Treasury to fix outdated systems go unanswered, the country shouldn't be surprised when it's cheated by fraudsters. It's the price we pay for big government and a Congress that's unable to do its job.

In the 90-Degree Turn, results take priority over principles. *"Life, liberty, and the pursuit of happiness"* takes a backseat to outcomes. Think of this as the mechanics of creating value, and not an attempt to subvert a democratic republic. Focusing on what is needed, and imagining how that need can be met, is a topic people can productively discuss. The problem today is that principles are reduced to political affiliation. When this is our starting point emotions dominate, dialog dies, and zero is accomplished. The same poison that stifles progress in Washington poisons the hearts and minds of Americans. At the door of doing better, we must learn to check our political affiliation in the hope of restoring Isaiah 1:18: *"Come now and let us reason together."*[104]

Aligning local and state government from the bottom-up, through a national *Needs Monitor,* is how we put local, state, and federal governments on the same path. In this bottom-up process, we cherry-pick government assets while identifying waste and redundancy.

Reasoning from First Principles

Finally, Greek philosophy (not just mythology) has found its place in space. In establishing his rocket company, SpaceX, Elon Musk applied Aristotle's *reasoning from first principles.*[105] Musk had an appreciation for what rockets could do but was confronted with the overwhelming task of building his own. Efforts to acquire Intercontinental Ballistic Missiles (ICBMs), minus their nuclear warheads, from Russia hadn't panned out. Musk was on his own.

---

[104] Isaiah 1:18 King James. Come now, and let us reason together, saith the LORD: though your sins be as scarlet, they shall be as white as snow; though they be red like crimson, they shall be as wool.

[105] "The first basis from which a thing is known." Aristotle, Metaphysics 1013a14-15

He did what had brought him success in the past and read every book he could find on rockets. Musk also dove into the details of a Russian rocket manual that had been translated into English. Using *reasoning from first principles,* Musk broke rockets into their smallest parts, to a point where they couldn't be broken down any further. No longer seeing a towering missile but rather millions of pieces: *"aerospace-grade aluminum alloys... titanium, copper, and carbon fiber."*[106] After calculating the cost of materials, Musk came to a profound realization. The cost of the materials that went into a rocket was only about two percent of the rocket's actual cost. The culprit, he realized, was the army of suppliers, and suppliers to suppliers, whose components made up a rocket. For each, there was the cost of the component they made or assembled, plus a profit margin. In addition, there were administrative costs for ordering and managing each component. With rockets having millions of parts, the cost of managing inventories is not trivial.

Musk realized NASA was budgeting many times what was actually needed to build a rocket. Therein he hit on the opportunity that became SpaceX.

The beauty of *reasoning from first principles* is not just about getting to the essence of things but, according to Musk, in breaking from *comparison by analogy* and the status quo.[107] For most of us, tomorrow's outlook doesn't vary from yesterday's. The past has gotten us to where we are today. Questioning tradition and common practice cause discomfort; it's best to leave well enough alone. We're comfortable with what we know, even when we hate it and see it fail. Were it not for our risk-averse shortcomings, we would have radicalized Washington ages ago.

---

[106] "First Principles: Elon Musk on the Power of Thinking for Yourself" by James Clear. https://jamesclear.com/first-principles
[107] "The First Principles Method Explained by Elon Musk" December 4, 2013. Innomind. Interview by Kevin Rose published to Youtube: https://www.youtube.com/watch?v=NV3sBlRgzTI&ab_channel=innomind

Reasoning from first principles enabled Musk to remove himself from existing biases he had about rockets. To build a new rocket he had to think anew and detach himself from past experiences. In the process, new opportunities emerged. Building in-house provided more than just cost savings, it enabled engineering possibilities that had previously been considered science fiction. With the launch of SpaceX's Falcon 9 on December 21, 2015, we witnessed the impossible: controlled vertical landing. Never before had a rocket's first stage returned to earth and landed. Rather than being discarded in the ocean, as had been NASA's practice, SpaceX built rockets to be recycled, saving millions of dollars and further driving down the cost of space travel.

Hard work combined with the genius of Aristotelian logic proved a win-win. In optimal form, Musk showed how theory and practice are applied in creating value and making the world a better place. What NASA had estimated at $3.9 billion ultimately cost SpaceX $390 million – ten percent of NASA's estimate – and this was before factoring in the savings derived from first stage reuse.[108]

Like a rocket, the Federal Government is complex and made up of millions of pieces. Aristotle's *reasoning from first principles* provides a framework for looking at those pieces, determining the value of each, and re-assembling them for use in the 21st Century. Instead of seeing the U.S. Federal Government as a collection of timeless institutions, in the 90-Degree Turn we assess Washington's bureaucracy at its lowest level, right down to the individual.

---

[108] "Falcon 9 Launch Vehicle NAFCOM Cost Estimates" NASA Associate Deputy Administrator for Policy. August 2011

The Value Gap

The difference between the value of a particular item or service, and the cost of providing that item or service, is what I call the *Value Gap*.[109] As shown in the illustration, in the case of Healthcare.gov, the value of the website conservatively estimated to cost $10 million, and the Federal Government's actual cost of $1.7

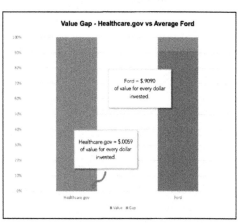

billion, equates to a *Value Gap* of 99.41%. In the case of the average Ford car (mentioned in Part II), the cost to build it is $20,000 while the cost to the consumer is $22,000. The Value Gap in this instance is 9.1%, which is Ford's well-earned gross profit.

The Value Gap between industry and government needs to narrow. Government may never be as efficient as industry; but half as efficient is a reasonable goal. This means reducing the government's Value Gap from 99.5% to about 20%.

The Affordable Care Act addressed a need, but at an outrageous cost. For every dollar spent, the taxpayer gets less than a penny of value in return. In rounded numbers, ninety-nine cents ($.99) on the dollar is Washington's overhead for providing a penny ($.01) of value derived from the Healthcare.gov website.

Despite its outlandish cost, Healthcare.gov provides a benefit to those seeking health insurance. Unfortunately, this cannot be said for the 2003 War in Iraq, when the

---

[109] The term "Value Gap" is used in various ways. Here it refers to the actual price (P) of an item or service and the cost (C) to provide it. In the case of Healthcare.gov the fair market price for the website as of 2013 was $10,000,000 ÷ $1,700,000,000 (its actual cost per I.G.) = 0.0058 − 1 = 0.9941.

mission's purpose to uncover Weapons of Mass Destruction (WMDs) was negated when none were found. By then the damage had already been done and the U.S. had committed itself to trillions in cost that provided nothing of value in return. Our leaders didn't take heed of General Powell's Pottery Barn rule: "*You break it, you own it.*"

The imminent threat to the U.S., a well-known certainty to some, didn't exist at all. Big spending is not just inefficient, it's reckless and the trigger to misguided war. The cost of the Iraq war is estimated at $2.4 trillion; some say the real cost is closer to $3 trillion.[110] In addition to this, trillions of dollars will eventually be spent to rebuild Iraq and repair and replenish U.S. military equipment used and lost during the war. For the Iraqi war, the Value Gap is negative. For every dollar spent in fighting it, at least another dollar is spent in undoing its damage. There's no accounting for the suffering and loss of life that resulted from the war, nor for estimating the cost of current and future lawsuits filed against the U.S. by the Iraqi government and Iraqi citizens. There's also the unknown impact of those with bitter memories: young boys who lost their fathers, whose only thought is revenge.

Despite its substantial Value Gap, compared to the inverse value of the 2003 Iraq war, Healthcare.gov is a winner.

When we work backwards from the end-goal, the cost of providing a service, a product, or an army is more likely to be proportional to the desired outcome. In the case of Healthcare.gov, the government created an insurance marketplace that has given Americans a place to shop and compare health insurance plans. Without Healthcare.gov we'd have to hunt for the best insurance plan by researching individual providers. That's

---

[110] The Three Trillion Dollar War By Joseph Stiglitz and Linda Bilmes. 2008.

more work than having a single web destination. But at what cost is the convenience of a health insurance portal justified? According to the U.S. Census Bureau, in 2020, 91.4% of the American population (300 million people) had healthcare insurance.[111] In the same year, the Centers for Medicare and Medicaid Services (CMS) reported that 3.6% of the population (12 million people) had utilized the Healthcare.gov website.[112] Had we rationally compared the expected outcome of helping Americans to find competitively priced healthcare insurance with the cost of providing a service to facilitate this need, it would have been obvious not to develop Healthcare.gov at all, even at its initial budget of $93.7 million.

The rollercoaster of politically driven decision-making, combined with legions of hungry contractors and lobbyists, has resulted in a lot the country never asked for.

Bottom-up Separation

Bottom-up separation should be seen as a revolution. Not one that overthrows government, but rather one that radically changes how government operates. The *Needs Monitor* is the compass that guides us in this change by aligning local requirements with State and Federal Government resources. Not produced by civil servants, contractors, or political leaders, the Needs Monitor is created locally by everyday citizens in towns and cities throughout the country. It's at the opposite end of Washington's governmental spectrum.

Here's a simple example of how it works.

Step One: SURVEY

---

[111] Health Insurance Coverage in the United States: 2020. U.S. Census Bureau

[112] Health Insurance Exchanges 2020 Open Enrollment Report April 1, 2020. CMS.gov

Take an issue like clean water. Suppose you live in Flint, Michigan and know that drinking water is contaminated with lead. As a citizen, you identify this as your top concern. You may have reported other issues, but "*clean lead-free drinkable water*" is at the top of your list. Other towns and cities in Michigan report their priorities too in the Needs Monitor. Clean drinkable water may not be a top concern for everyone in Michigan, but it is likely a top concern for thousands.

Step Two: PROPOSE

Based on the information collected from citizens via the Needs Monitor, the State of Michigan formulates a request for proposal (RFP) to the Federal Government. In it, they explain the problem, provide background information, and outline specifically what they need. Every state knows how to write an RFP so this is a process that should come relatively easy. Michigan's RFP, which could be joined by other states, is shared with the Federal Government. The Commerce Business Daily (CBD), or something like it, which advertises government procurements to the country, could be used to advertise Michigan's RFP to the Federal Government.

Step Three: RESPOND

Once submitted to Washington, any department in the Federal Government can respond to Michigan's RFP. There can also be collaborative efforts where teams from different agencies and departments of the Federal Government work together. This is encouraged. Members of Congress can help facilitate this process by turning their attention away from politicking to connecting Washington's resources with the needs of their constituencies.

In Step Three *separation* comes into play. In the process of the Federal Government responding to state issued RFPs, we see which Washington assets are in demand. We also see how many departments in the Federal Government can address those demands, and where there's redundancy. On some matters, like national defense, a level of redundancy is needed. The same can be said for protecting the public from nuclear waste. If one system fails, others need to kick in. That's redundancy with a purpose and not the result of bloated government. Currently, however, there are many instances where redundancies exist without a purpose, other than to spend. One department is doing the same work as other departments. Contractors can be the source of redundancy too, paid to mirror an agency's work. In separation, redundancies are identified and either repurposed or removed.

These 3 steps, *Survey*, *Propose*, and *Respond*, form the cycle through which the needs of the country are processed. By iterating through each, we engage in the governmental equivalent of *reasoning from first principles*. We break government down to its smallest working components and then rebuild it. Gradually, a new government emerges, grounded to the needs of the country rather than a political agenda. We have the tools in front of us to better represent ourselves, our family, our community, and our country. Connecting local needs with Federal Government resources forms the hinge that enables Washington to pivot.

In addition to collecting and organizing the country's requirements, the Needs Monitor also tracks results. No longer will we need a Congressional hearing to see what is in plain view. As progress is monitored and measured, governments will be driven by the collective wisdom of the country instead of the preferences of a select few.

In the Michigan example, people who voice concern for water quality in the Needs Monitor will see where similar problems exist in their state and the country. Solutions being tested in one town or city can be freely compared to solutions tested elsewhere. As a platform for reporting local requirements, citizens are encouraged to offer solutions too in the Needs Monitor. In this bottom-up approach the collective know-how of the country will do a lot to inform and shape local and federal government. It's an opportunity for us to tap into the ingenuity of others and the resourcefulness of everyday Americans.

Below is an illustration of the current U.S. Federal Government. Across the top are 15 columns that represent its primary agencies. Down the side are 27 rows that represent the combined size of departments within these 15 agencies. We have what looks like an elongated checkerboard representing the 403 different agencies and departments of the Federal Government. It's here that Washington's bureaucracy spends one-third of the country's GDP, roughly $7 trillion annually. Receipts from taxes and fees only cover about half this amount; the difference is added to the national debt.

As the needs of the country cycle through Step 1, 2, and 3, we create a profile of the Federal Government that aligns with the country. In the process we identify the Federal Government's most and least needed resources. In the illustration, a blank indicates *no interest*, light grey is *some interest*, dark grey *a lot of interest*, and black *a must-have*.

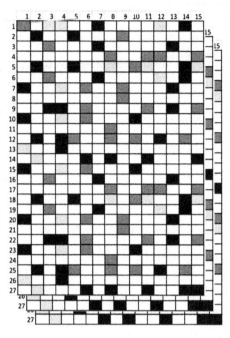

Agencies / Departments of the U.S. Federal Government

Executive Office of the President (9)

Executive Departments (15)

Executive Department Sub-Agencies and Bureaus (260)

Independent Agencies (66)

Boards, Commissions, and Committees (42)

Quasi-Official Agencies (11)

Total: 403 agencies and departments – a workforce of 9.8 million.

Of course, this illustration is an oversimplification. Given that the Federal Government employs 9.8 million people (including contractors) we need to imagine this grid running many layers deep and off the page. Nevertheless, through the process of *Survey, Propose,* and *Respond* we begin to define a new Washington – one tied to the local needs of citizens.

Voting accomplishes one thing but is static compared to a system that records needs, monitors progress, and provides the ability for everyday Americans to offer solutions. It's a chance for millions of citizens to lend a hand in rebuilding the country. *"Ask not what your country can do for you, ask what you can do for your country,"* may, once again, find a place in the U.S.[113]

---

[113] President Kennedy, 1961 inaugural address

Consider Amazon. The key to its success is providing an efficient connection between what consumers need and what vendors produce. Amazon uses data and automation to match needs with resources. They also continuously monitor performance to identify areas for improvement. Amazon's approach is analogous to using the Needs Monitor to determine which programs should be funded and monitoring how well those funds are spent. While government and Amazon have vastly different missions, a lot can be derived from Amazon's success that can help guide the hand of future state and federal governments. Not doing so is equivalent to government thumbing its nose to the future. As Jefferson argued, government must adapt to the times and avail itself to current circumstances. Government has a history but shouldn't be tied down by it.

While separating waste from wants, the Needs Monitor helps the country separate itself from the warfare of political affiliation. Blinded by political ire, we rarely get to the point of *reasoning together*. What if the country did the important things and simply addressed its needs and ignored the labels of affiliation: Democrat, Republican, and Independent? By focusing on tangible and validated local and national needs we cancel political noise and get on with the business of solving problems. In the Needs Monitor there's no field for party affiliation. The only affiliation that matters is being a citizen of the United States of America.

Change Management

Change is inevitable when excuses run out. Up to a point, it's easier to rationalize the government's poor performance than it is to fix it. Two hundred thirty-three years of history, and nearly a century of economic and military dominance, is hard to argue. The thought of interfering with this legacy is a discomforting one. Staying the course, and hoping for a better tomorrow, is an easier path. Like a canoe being slowly pulled toward a waterfall, the sensation of imminent danger escapes us.

A look at the past twenty years should be enough to scare us into action. An unimaginable plunge is just ahead. The frustration of millions of Americans – across the entire political spectrum – is not an illusion and not without cause.

Creating Urgency is Step 1 in the model developed by renowned change management expert John P. Kotter. Living in a world of non-stop *breaking news,* we should be comfortable with the topic of urgency. Of course, "breaking news" is often not real urgency, but rather mass media's artificial signal that keeps us hooked enough to check back or click back, over and over.

The real pending urgency can be better grasped if we imagine the U.S. as a developing nation where people earn less, live worse, and beg in retirement. We see it already, but at a low level compared to what it will become. During a winter trip to Moscow in 1995, I saw an old woman standing outside a subway station. She held a used car battery in her bare hands. It was her ticket to heating and some bread. The old woman was not alone but one in a long row of Russian pensioners lined up along the metro entrance. Living on fixed incomes during a period of hyperinflation that reached 197 percent that year was pushing retired Russians to the brink.[114] Many good people who spent a lifetime working now stood in the frigid cold hoping to sell whatever they could, just to get by. In their old and wrinkled faces, I saw desperation and disbelief. How had this happened? How can this be? How am I to survive? In addition to everyday hardships, hundreds went blind or

---

[114] International Monetary Fund, International Financial Statistics and data files.

dropped dead because they could no longer afford state-made vodka and had to resort to the cheap stuff, often concocted with antifreeze.

Minus the Russian winter, some see scenes like this already in America. No doubt it will be the future for many Americans unless we decide to act. American exceptionalism is of no value as a concept. If not practiced in earnest, it doesn't exist.

After Creating Urgency, the next 7 steps form the rest of Kotter's model. Each of these can be applied in executing the 90-Degree Turn theory, as noted in my *comments*.

Step 2: Form a Powerful <u>Coalition</u> – *People determined to significantly improve government form a powerful coalition.*

Step 3: Create a <u>Vision</u> for Change – *Separation – as illustrated in the above example – is the vision for what the Federal Government should look like at any given time.*

Step 4: <u>Communicate</u> the Vision – *This book is the starting point. It defines the problems we face in Washington (and particularly with Congress) and puts forward a framework and mechanisms for returning value to government. The theory is not intended to answer every question or address every matter in Washington. Doing so would just repeat Washington's mistake. Better is to act, measure, refine, and repeat.*

Step 5: Remove <u>Obstacles</u> – *Time, indifference, and inaction are the obstacles in front of us. The urgency of this matter should enable us to overcome these.*

Step 6: Create Short-Term Wins – *Removing Congress's grip on money will be a significant short-term win. Of equal importance is showing how the 90-Degree Turn aligns government with needs to create value.*

Step 7: Build on the Change – *As we peel back the layers of government, better approaches emerge. Bottom-up separation goes from revolutionary to business as usual. Not a one-off but an ongoing way of identifying and streamlining Washington (and State) resources and applying those resources where they offer the greatest value.*

Step 8: Anchor the Changes to the Country's Culture – *With exceptionalism practiced, not preached, we not only redefine our Federal Government but provide a model for hundreds of others.*

A velvet revolution of sorts, the 90-Degree Turn must be executed in stages to work. It's only in this way that lean management principles can be applied. In the process of identifying and aligning state and federal governments with the needs of citizens, we measure. Not just to assess the effectiveness of an outcome but also to quantify the steps involved in reaching that outcome.

The Founding Fathers didn't have the benefit of the knowledge, skills, and tools we possess today. While we share their ideology, we seem to forget they were revolutionaries. They didn't wait for things to happen, but made things happen. If I imagine myself in the company of Franklin or Jefferson today, I can hear them asking: "*What are we waiting for?*"

EPILOGUE

I wrote this book in the hope of finding a way to restore the promise of the world's first and oldest democratic republic, the United States of America. While our core principles – life, liberty, and the pursuit of happiness – are as purposeful today as in 1787, the government charged with upholding these principles is in peril.

Complexity and *size*, largely a result of the U.S.'s old age, are the ailments of the Federal Government that clog the country's arteries, make us ill, and induce pain. In the hands of a fundraising-centric Congress, these conditions become life-threatening. The danger is not just the debt that has increased five-times in twenty years ($5.6 trillion to over $30 trillion) but, to a greater extent, Washington's gross inefficiency, recklessness, and hypocrisy.

As Federal Government spending now accounts for one-third of the U.S. economy, change must come quickly but incrementally. We want to transform the Federal Government, not destroy it, or add to its dysfunction. By taking a bottom-up approach, we remake government while giving every American a direct voice in prioritizing the country's needs. In the process, our legacy top-down governance model is turned on its head.

Not only does this approach help federal and state governments to align with the needs of citizens, but it also works as a filter that identifies waste, inefficiency, and redundancy. In aligning needs with resources that produce solutions, we streamline – pivoting to a government that's measured by its accountability to the citizens of the United States of America.

While the 90-Degree Turn provides a model for streamlining Washington's bureaucracy, its most drastic measure is reserved for Congress. As the gatekeepers of the country's spending, Congress has demonstrated that it can no longer uphold this all-important responsibility. For this reason, budget and spending authorization should be removed from Washington and delegated to state governments. This isn't an acknowledgment of state government efficiency as much as a declaration of Congress's profound failure and the need for urgent action. By uncoupling Washington politicians and budgets, we put a hole in fundraising-centric politics. Compensating donors through contract awards and legislation will be more difficult when funding decisions are grounded in locally validated needs, not party ideology and back-room dealings.

Of course, unfavorable and illegal dealings will continue as long as humans run government. However, by removing Congress from its economic chokehold on the nation and focusing on local needs, fundraising-centric politics are largely neutralized. Instead of the usual, Congress's focus changes to the bottom-up reorientation of the country with State and Federal Government assets. Future members of Congress may be lawyers, but they should also be managers, skilled at building teams and getting things done. We can transform Congress from a world of words to one of results.

As a central body, it would seem more efficient to have Congress debate and approve the country's budget instead of delegating this responsibility to state governments. For a long time, the centralized approach worked well. Unfortunately, this is no longer the case. As political rhetoric goes hyperbolic, so does political divide and the national debt. In Washington, progress is in reverse.

In the 90-Degree Turn, Congress is not dissolved but rebooted and tasked with linking the Federal Government's vast resources with the needs of the constituency they serve. Additionally, rather than legislating new laws, Congress will work to simplify existing laws, based on local needs. They will also be tasked with streamlining tax code to reduce costs and stimulate economic growth. Reducing tax preparation from 14% of tax receipts to 1% saves the average taxpayer over $1,000; going from $1,081 to $77.[115] If we were to follow Europe's approach, we could reduce the cost of a tax return to pennies.[116] Simplifying law and utilizing nudges over mandates returns value to government and makes for a happier, more productive, and affluent population.

As a nation of fifty states, the U.S. has the advantage of being inherently decentralized. When the Federal Government fails, the States are our backup plan. As with any pivot, the road will be bumpy at first as we detour from common ground in the pursuit of something better. Despite this, our detour is not an option but a must if we are to avoid the imminent disaster that is today's U.S. Federal Government. As Washington's value is restored, fiscal authority can be returned to Congress. But, given the work in front of us, this will likely be a decade or more in the making.

---

[115] In 2019, taxpayers filed 148.3 million tax returns at an approximate cost of $153 billion or $1,081 per return.

In closing, let me remind you that what I provided in this book is a theory. It's incomplete and short on details. I want to get into those details, but I thought it wise to sell the concept first. That's the goal of this book. If we don't break from "comparison by analogy," as Musk professes, new approaches to democracy will be rejected from the outset and never make it to the slow (thinking) part of our brain. I realize this knee-jerk tendency, particularly concerning the highly charged topic of politics in America. I suffer from this condition too. Don't we all?

Like life itself, there are 99 reasons for this theory to fail and only one reason for it to succeed: our determination to do better.

Before giving into our present-day temptation to attack, trash, and kill, try sleeping on the ideas described in this book. Are there any aspects of the theory that have merit? What would you recommend for making it better?

In my experience, success is an iterative process. We begin with an idea and work through it, refining it in each step. At the start, good rules over perfect. Of course, we want perfect, but we know it takes many good steps before we even get a glimpse of it. It's then that we realize that perfect is not just about results but our determination to do better.

Many years ago, I heard a psychologist who was counseling a patient for depression say: "don't think yourself into better action, act yourself into better thinking." My book is an attempt, and a beginning, at helping us to act ourselves into better thinking and better government for the future of democracy in the United States of America and around the world.

If you're interested in following this theory and contributing to its formation, email me at jbfred.eberlein@gmail.com. I look forward to getting your feedback and, eventually, to turning the 90-Degree Turn into a working model.

I want to thank my brother Bobby for his help in writing this book. While we share a common outlook on life, our views can differ widely on government and politics. It was in this regard that his feedback and insights were most beneficial. Bobby didn't just accept this theory because it came from his older brother but questioned it each step of the way, just as I wanted. In so doing, he made this work better. Without his active participation this book would tell a different story.

Also, a special thanks to my editors, Felicity Dippery and Michael Hirsch, for their exceptional work.

Made in the USA
Middletown, DE
25 January 2023

23091137R00070